Best Easy Day Hikes
Portland, Maine

Help Us Keep This Guide Up to Date

Every effort has been made by the author and editors to make this guide as accurate and useful as possible. However, many things can change after a guide is published—campgrounds open and close, grow and contract; regulations change; facilities come under new management; and so forth.

We welcome your comments concerning your experiences with this guide and how you feel it could be improved and kept up to date. While we may not be able to respond to all comments and suggestions, we'll take them to heart, and we'll also make certain to share them with the author. Please send your comments and suggestions to the following address:

> FalconGuides
> Reader Response/Editorial Department
> 246 Goose Lane
> Guilford, CT 06437

Or you may e-mail us at:

> editorial@falcon.com

Thanks for your input, and happy trails!

Best Easy Day Hikes Series

Best Easy Day Hikes
Portland, Maine

Greg Westrich

FALCON GUIDES

GUILFORD, CONNECTICUT
HELENA, MONTANA

FALCONGUIDES®

An imprint of Rowman & Littlefield
Falcon and FalconGuides are registered trademarks and Make
Adventure Your Story is a trademark of Rowman & Littlefield.

Distributed by NATIONAL BOOK NETWORK

Copyright © 2016 by Rowman & Littlefield

Maps © Rowman & Littlefield

British Library Cataloguing-in-Publication Information Available

Library of Congress Cataloging-in-Publication Data Available.

ISBN 978-1-4930-1664-8 (paperback)
ISBN 978-1-4930-2391-2 (e-book)

∞™ The paper used in this publication meets the minimum
requirements of American National Standard for Information
Sciences—Permanence of Paper for Printed Library Materials, ANSI/
NISO Z39.48-1992.

Front cover photo: The mouth of the Kennebec River protected by
Fort Popham. Back cover photo: The Blue Trail at Hamilton Audubon
Sanctuary.

Contents

Acknowledgments... viii
Introduction 1
   Wildlife.. 3
   Bugs... 4
   Plant Life 5
   Weather and Seasons.. 5
   Be Prepared 7
   Zero Impact.. 9
How to Use This Guide... 10
Trail Finder 11
Map Legend... 14

The Hikes

  1. Cutts Island.. 15
  2. Vaughan Woods 19
  3. Mount Agamenticus 24
  4. Kennebunk Plains.. 28
  5. Carson Trail 32
  6. Timber Point... 36
  7. Saco Heath 40
  8. Douglas Mountain.. 44
  9. Mount Cutler 48
10. Burnt Meadow Mountain 52
11. Two Lights State Park..................................... 56
12. Rattlesnake Mountain 60
13. Wolfe's Neck Woods 64
14. Bradbury Mountain... 70
15. Long Reach Preserve....................................... 75
16. Harpswell Cliffs 79
17. Giant's Stairs 83
18. Hamilton Audubon Sanctuary 87

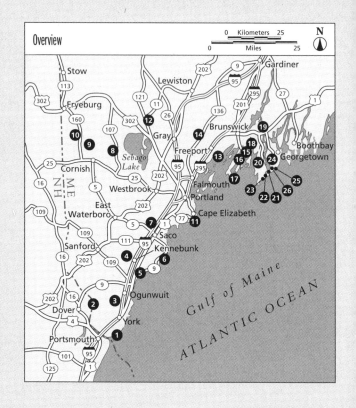

19. Thorne Head 91
20. Sprague Pond Loop 95
21. Cox's Head 99
22. Spirit Pond 103
23. Seawall Beach 107
24. Higgins Mountain 111
25. Josephine Newman Sanctuary 115
26. Berry Woods 119

Hike Index 123
About the Author 124

Acknowledgments

When I was eight, my parents took me and my two younger brothers on our first camping trip in a borrowed tent. It rained the whole weekend. What I remember most about the trip was standing in a light mist beneath drooping white pines. A great horned owl dropped from a nearby tree and floated silently between the rusty trunks and out of sight. I want to thank my folks, Larry and Dianne Westrich, for giving me that experience and the hundreds of others that followed on our many family vacations. It was those childhood moments of wonder and awe that lit my hiking bug.

Introduction

Maine's Southern Coast is a typical coastal plain: long sweeping beaches separated by prominent headlands backed by a relatively flat plain. This geography is typical of much of the Atlantic Coast south of Maine. In New England, as the Appalachian Mountains bend toward the coast, the breadth of the coastal plain narrows—and almost disappears east of Portland. The Casco Bay region transitions from sandy beaches to the rockbound coast of the rest of Maine. The transition has less to do with a change in bedrock and more to do with the direction of the bedding in relation to the coast. Along the coast south of Casco Bay, the bedrock is laid down parallel to the shoreline. At Casco Bay the coast begins to bend to the east, and the bedrock juts out nearly perpendicular into the ocean.

There are few major rivers in the region south of Portland but numerous small streams that flow through lowland woods and salt marshes on their short journeys to the sea. The Mousam River, for example, flows 26 miles from Mousam Lake in Shapleigh to the river's mouth in Kennebunkport. Along the way it flows past farms, through woods and salt marshes. The river remains surprisingly wild. A hike along its bank in the woods of the Kennebunk Plains or an exploration of its mouth at Parsons Beach can attest to that.

North of Portland the southern Mid-Coast is dominated by two rivers: the Kennebec and the Adroscoggin. They flow together, forming Merrymeeting Bay many miles inland. The rocky peninsulas and islands near the Kennebec's mouth receive the rivers load of silt, creating some of Maine's best beaches.

There are few mountains near the coast but a number of promontories with views, such as Mount Agamenticus and Bradbury Mountain. Both of these are granite, although there is little granite along the Southern Coast. In several places along the Southern Coast, granite has been intruded into the gaps in older, usually sedimentary, rock. It makes for some interesting formations; the shore on the east side of Wolfe's Neck and Giant's Stairs are good examples.

Farther inland the land rises and becomes quite mountainous. There are many fine mountain hikes within an hour's drive of Portland. From many of them you can see the higher mountains of western Maine and New Hampshire's White Mountains.

Changes in sea level during and after the last ice age have left their mark in the Portland region. During the last ice age, the sea level was much lower. But because the ice depressed the bedrock, right after the ice age, the coast was much farther inland than it is today. The ice melted—and raised the sea level—faster than the bedrock rebounded. There are places along the Southern Coast where sand beaches can be found miles inland. The Kennebunk Plains and the commercial attraction in Freeport called the Desert of Maine are examples.

Greater Portland is a little more than 10 percent of the state's area, but has more than a third of the people. The region is much more developed than any other part of Maine. Only in southern Maine are sprawl and disappearing wildlands a serious concern. There are many local land trusts working to keep some of the land wild. Most of the protected tracts are small with walking paths, not hiking trails. Similarly, the beaches and state parks along the Southern Coast are best suited for day use and recreation, not hiking.

Even so, it is surprising how much wildness still exists within a short drive of Portland, and how much hiking you can do. This guide is an introduction to the region's variety.

Wildlife

By weight there are more salamanders in Maine than moose—which is another way of saying that most wildlife isn't big but small. You won't see any large mammals hiking near Portland, but you will—if you look around—see plenty of wildlife. There are moose, coyotes, and bears living in southern Maine, especially inland, but they are far less common than in the North Woods.

Dozens of species of amphibians are out there for you to find. It's not uncommon to see a half-dozen different kinds of frogs and toads on a hike. Maine also has several kinds of snakes—none poisonous—that often sun on warm trails.

Maine is also home to numerous weasels and rodents. You are unlikely to see a stoat or fisher, but you would be hard-pressed to take a hike free of squirrels. They sit on downfall or in trees, commenting loudly on passing hikers. Beavers are common in Maine's lakes and streams. Their handiwork is easy to find, but seeing one of the shy rodents is less likely. They are most active in the twilight of early morning and late evening. Be on the lookout for porcupines. During the day they can often be found sleeping in trees near where they've been feeding.

Maine's coast is a magnet for birders because of the diverse habitats and the presence of northern species not found elsewhere in the United States. Birdsong is a constant presence on hikes, whether it's the chatter of a family of chickadees, the musical song of a hermit thrush, or the cry of a circling osprey. Your ears will find many more birds than your eyes. A few of the hikes in this guide pass very near active osprey nests. The best birding is during spring and fall migrations, but the coast offers seabirds and ducks that come from the north for the relatively milder climate and protected waters along Maine's bays and estuaries.

Bugs

One theory holds that Maine is so sparsely populated because of the biting insects. They can be quite annoying—even ruin an otherwise great day of hiking. There are blackflies, checker flies, moose flies, no-see-ums, mosquitoes, and, recently, ticks. Blackflies are worst between Mother's Day and Father's Day but are around all summer. They are only active during the day. Blackfly saliva numbs your skin, so you often aren't aware of all your bites until they start bleeding and itching. Over time blackfly bites seem to cause less swelling and itching, as if the immune system learns to fight back. Even so, when they are at their worst, many Mainers wear a bug net over their head for protection.

Mosquitoes are active day and night, and are most common in cool, damp areas—which means that unless there's snow on the ground, there is something out there wanting to bite you. Always carry bug dope. Having said that, you will have many bug-free hiking days, especially when it's breezy.

In 2013 when I hiked 800 miles for *Hiking Maine*, I got exactly one tick. In 2014 I hiked less than 200 miles for *Best Easy Day Hikes Camden, Maine* and got too many ticks to count. On one hike—that didn't make the book—I removed more than forty ticks from my legs. In 2014 and 2015, hiking for *Best Easy Day Hikes Portland, Maine,* I had a few ticks. Ticks are most common in tall grass. After hiking through a meadow or open area, you should check yourself for ticks and remove any before they get a chance to attach.

Plant Life

Tourists flock to New England in the fall for the foliage. It's well worth the trip, but what many people—even native Mainers—miss are the spring colors. When the trees begin to leaf out, the mountainsides are awash in varying shades of green with reds and yellows thrown in. Maybe it's not as dramatic as in the fall, but beautiful just the same. Beneath the trees a profusion of wildflowers rush to bloom before the canopy closes and leaves them in the shade for the summer.

Through the summer a succession of berries ripen for hikers to snack on. Especially prized are blueberries. Good blueberry spots are noted in this guide. The blueberries usually begin to ripen in mid- to late July. When you're suffering through the blackflies early in the summer, remember them as you are munching on trailside blueberries: Blackflies are an important blueberry pollinator.

In the fall, beneath the vibrant trees, there is an explosion of mushrooms. At least a thousand varieties of fungi are native to Maine. Most of the time they live unobserved within the soil, in rotting vegetation, and on tree roots. But in the fall they bloom: Fungi send up fruiting bodies that release spoors—like tiny seeds—into the air. We call these fruiting bodies mushrooms.

Weather and Seasons

You hear a lot of Mainers say that if you don't like the weather, wait five minutes and it'll change. Of course, that's an exaggeration, but not by much. On any given day the weather across the state can vary widely. In general it's cooler, milder, and breezier along the coast. The Maine coast is among the foggiest places on Earth, but don't let that keep you off the trails. Hiking in the fog can be a wonderful experience. In winter, when most of the state is buried under deep snow, you can hike near the coast. You just have to be careful of ice. Often the milder weather along the coast leaves trails sheened with ice instead of snow.

Some of the hikes in this book are inaccessible in winter. Before you head out, check the individual trail description for access. Hiking in the winter—with or without snowshoes—can be extra work, but is often worth the effort. Maine in winter offers great solitude and beautiful landscapes.

Spring is mud season in Maine, and trails are often muddy and wet. Still, spring hiking is wonderful. Wildflowers are beginning to emerge, the birds are singing, and there are no bugs yet.

Summer more than triples the population of Maine. There are more summer homes here than in any other state. Most of the tourists and summer people congregate along the coast and in the towns, especially after July 4. Even so, most of the hikes never get crowded. Even when US 1 is bumper-to-bumper traffic, you can find solitude on a hike most days. It rarely gets hotter than the mid-80s, but you still need to be prepared for hot, dry conditions in the summer.

Fall can be the best time for hiking: The summer crowds are gone, the weather is cooler, and after the first freeze, the bugs are gone. And then there's the fall colors. The colors in southern Maine are less showy than farther north—the oaks that dominate many of the region's forests aren't as vibrant as maples. Most years you can hike right up until around

Thanksgiving without having to worry much about snow. It can and does snow as early as late September, though, so bring appropriate clothing and gear.

To be safe, no matter what the season or the weather when you start a hike, assume it will change. Always bring a jacket and raincoat, even on the warmest summer day. In spring and fall it's good to layer, so you can put on and take off layers as needed. Remember: It's best to start out cool; sweat is the enemy. Except in the summer, avoid cotton clothes. Cotton is comfortable, but when it gets wet or sweaty, it can be cold, even dangerously so. Adding a few things to your pack just in case may make the climbs a little tougher, but in the long run will make your hikes safer and more comfortable.

Maine's weather is not something to complain about; rather, it's to be prepared for and then enjoyed in all its various manifestations. The bottom line is that in Maine every season and every kind of weather can make for great hiking.

Be Prepared

Hiking in the Portland, Maine, area is generally safe. Still, hikers should be prepared. Some specific advice:

Know the basics of first aid, including how to treat bleeding, bites and stings, and fractures, strains, or sprains. Pack a first-aid kit on every excursion.

Familiarize yourself with the symptoms of heat exhaustion and heat stroke. Heat exhaustion symptoms include heavy sweating, muscle cramps, headache, dizziness, and fainting. Should you or any of your hiking party exhibit any of these symptoms, cool the victim down immediately by rehydrating and getting him or her to an air-conditioned location. Cold showers also help reduce body temperature.

Heat stroke is much more serious: The skin is hot and dry to the touch, and the victim may lose consciousness. In this event, call 911 immediately.

Regardless of the weather, your body needs a lot of water while hiking. A full 32-ounce bottle is the minimum for these short hikes, but more is always better. Bring a full water bottle, whether water is available along the trail or not.

Don't drink from streams, rivers, creeks, or lakes without treating or filtering the water first. Waterways and water bodies may host a variety of contaminants, including giardia, which can cause serious intestinal unrest.

Prepare for extremes of both heat and cold by dressing in layers.

Carry a backpack in which you can store extra clothing, ample drinking water and food, and whatever goodies, like guidebooks, cameras, and binoculars, you might want. Consider bringing a GPS with tracking capabilities.

Cell phone coverage is widespread, but you can never be absolutely sure until you are on location. Bring your device, but make sure you've turned it off or got it on the vibrate setting while hiking. Nothing like a "wake the dead"–loud ring to startle every creature, including fellow hikers.

Keep children under careful watch. Trails travel along lakes, creeks, tidal streams, and the ocean, some of which are not recommended for swimming. Hazards along some of the trails include poison ivy, uneven footing, and tidal muck; make sure children don't stray from the designated route. Children should carry a plastic whistle; if they become lost, they should stay in one place and blow the whistle to summon help.

Zero Impact

We, as trail users, must be especially vigilant to make sure our passage leaves no lasting mark. Here are some basic guidelines for preserving trails in the region:

Pack out all your own trash, including biodegradable items like orange peels. You might also pack out garbage left by less considerate hikers.

Don't approach or feed any wild creatures—the ground squirrel eyeing your snack food is best able to survive if it remains self-reliant.

Don't pick wildflowers or gather rocks, shells, feathers, and other treasures along the trail, especially aboriginal and settler relics. Removing these items will only take away from the next hiker's experience.

Avoid damaging trailside soils and plants by remaining on the established route. This is also a good rule of thumb for avoiding poison ivy and other common regional trailside irritants.

Be courteous by not making loud noises while hiking.

Many of these trails are multiuse, which means you'll share them with other hikers, trail runners, mountain bikers, and equestrians. Familiarize yourself with the proper trail etiquette, yielding the trail when appropriate.

Use outhouses at trailheads or along the trail.

How to Use This Guide

You'll find the quick, nitty-gritty details of the hike, such as where the trailhead is located, total hike length, approximate hiking time, difficulty rating, type of trail terrain, best hiking season, other trail users you may encounter, whether a fee is required, and trail contacts (for updates on trail conditions). The "Finding the trailhead" section gives you dependable directions from the Maine Turnpike (I-95) or I-295 right down to where you'll want to park your car. The hike description is the meat of the chapter, where you'll get a more detailed description of the trail. In "Miles and Directions" mileage cues identify all turns and trail name changes, as well as points of interest.

Trail Finder

Best Hikes for Coast Lovers

1. Cutts Island
6. Timber Point
11. Two Lights State Park
13. Wolfe's Neck Woods
15. Long Reach Preserve
17. Giant's Stairs
18. Hamilton Audubon Sanctuary
19. Thorne Head
21. Cox's Head
23. Seawall Beach
25. Josephine Newman Sanctuary
26. Berry Woods

Best Hikes for Geology Lovers

3. Mount Agamenticus
4. Kennebunk Plains
8. Douglas Mountain
9. Mount Cutler
11. Two Lights State Park
14. Bradbury Mountain
16. Harpswell Cliffs
17. Giant's Stairs
24. Higgins Mountain
25. Josephine Newman Sanctuary

Best Hikes for Birders

1. Cutts Island
2. Vaughan Woods
4. Kennebunk Plains

5. Carson Trail

6. Timber Point

7. Saco Heath

13. Wolfe's Neck Woods

17. Giant's Stairs

22. Spirit Pond

25. Josephine Newman Sanctuary

26. Berry Woods

Best Hikes for **Swimming**

1. Cutts Island

5. Carson Trail

6. Timber Point

11. Two Lights State Park

13. Wolfe's Neck Woods

23. Seawall Beach

Best Hikes for **History**

2. Vaughan Woods

3. Mount Agamenticus

8. Douglas Mountain

11. Two Lights State Park

13. Wolfe's Neck Woods

19. Thorne Head

21. Cox's Head

Best Hikes for **Children**

1. Cutts Island

4. Kennebunk Plains

5. Carson Trail

6. Timber Point

7. Saco Heath

11. Two Lights State Park

13. Wolfe's Neck Woods

14. Bradbury Mountain
16. Harpswell Cliffs
17. Giant's Stairs
19. Thorne Head
21. Cox's Head
23. Seawall Beach
24. Higgins Mountain
25. Josephine Newman Sanctuary
26. Berry Woods

Best Hikes for Great Views

3. Mount Agamenticus
6. Timber Point
8. Douglas Mountain
9. Mount Cutler
10. Burnt Meadow Mountain
12. Rattlesnake Mountain
14. Bradbury Mountain
15. Long Reach Preserve
16. Harpswell Cliffs
17. Giant's Stairs
21. Cox's Head
22. Spirit Pond
23. Seawall Beach
24. Higgins Mountain

Map Legend

〰95〰	Interstate Highway
〰1〰	US Highway
〰9〰	State Highway
═══	Local Road
= = = =	Unpaved Road
├──┼──┤	Railroad
‖‖‖‖‖‖	Boardwalk
▬▬▬▬	Featured Trail
- - - - -	Trail
- ·· - ·· -	State Border
〜	River/Stream
⬭	Body of Water
≈≈≈	Marsh
▭	State/County/Preserve/Wilderness
■	Building/Point of Interest
†	Cemetery
⊼	Lighthouse
✗	Mine
▲	Mountain/Peak
🅿	Parking
♿	Restroom
✿	Scenic View/Viewpoint
🗼	Tower
➓	Trailhead
≋	Waterfall

1 Cutts Island

The Cutts Island Trail follows tidal Chauncey Creek, which meanders through a wide salt marsh. The trail ends at an overlook of the marsh and Brave Boat Harbor beyond. The return hike remains inland, following a low hill through mixed hardwoods.

Start: Cutts Island Trailhead on north side of Seapoint Road just east of bridge over Chauncey Creek

Distance: 2.1-mile loop

Approximate hiking time: 2 hours

Difficulty: Easy

Best season: Apr–Oct

Trail surface: Woodland path

Land status: Rachel Carson National Wildlife Refuge

Nearest town: York Village

Other users: None

Water availability: None

Canine compatibility: No dogs allowed

Fees and permits: None

Maps: *DeLorme: Maine Atlas & Gazetteer* map 1; USGS Kittery

Trail contact: Rachel Carson National Wildlife Refuge, (207) 646-9226, www.fws.gov/refuge/rachel_carson

Finding the trailhead: From exit 7 on the Maine Turnpike (I-95), drive 0.4 mile to US 1. Turn right onto US 1 and drive 0.3 mile. Turn left onto US 1A and drive 1.4 miles. Turn left onto ME 103 and drive 4.1 miles. Turn left onto Cutts Island Lane and drive 0.3 mile to a T-intersection. Turn left onto Seapoint Road. You will immediately cross the bridge over Chauncey Creek. The trailhead is on the left just past the bridge. GPS: N43 05.273' / W70 40.529'

The Hike

Cutts Island isn't really an island. It is a high, wooded area bounded by salt marshes and the coast. But especially at high tide, you have the feeling of being on an island as you hike along Chauncey Creek. The creek is popular with kayakers, but you will likely have the woods to yourself.

The trail is part of the Brave Boat Harbor Unit of the Rachel Carson Wildlife Refuge. The refuge is more than 14,000 acres in several units spread out along the Maine coast from Kittery to Cape Elizabeth. It was established in 1966 to protect the habitat for migratory birds. In spring and fall, you are likely to at least hear several species of warblers in the woods. Out in the salt marshes and on the water, you may find several species of waterbirds. Eagles and ospreys are not uncommon visitors.

In the woods you may see New England cottontail rabbits—one of the reasons the hike doesn't allow dogs. This species of rabbit thrived in the abandoned farms of New England, but as that disused farmland returns to forest or became subdivisions, the cottontails are becoming rare. They are currently a candidate for listing as an endangered species.

From the end of the trail, you can look across the salt marsh and watch waves roll across Brave Boat Harbor. The sound of the surf hushes across the wind-tossed grasses.

After your hike you may want to continue down Seapoint Road to Seapoint Beach. Like many Maine beaches, it is as much gravel as sand but quite picturesque.

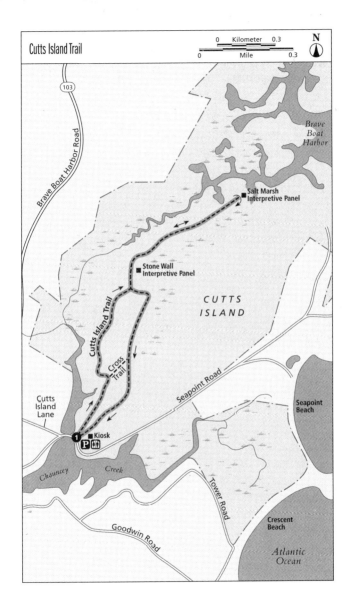

Cutts Island Trail

0 Kilometer 0.3
0 Mile 0.3

N

Brave Boat Harbor Road

103

Brave Boat Harbor

Salt Marsh Interpretive Panel

Stone Wall Interpretive Panel

CUTTS ISLAND

Cutts Island Trail

Cross Trail

Cutts Island Lane

Seapoint Road

Seapoint Beach

1 Kiosk
P

Chauncey Creek

Tower Road

Crescent Beach

Goodwin Road

Atlantic Ocean

Miles and Directions

0.0 Start from the trailhead on the north side of Seapoint Road east of the bridge over Chauncey Creek. Follow the trail along the creek, to the left of the restroom.

0.2 Bear left as you pass the Cross Trail.

0.3 The trail leaves Chauncey Creek.

0.5 Turn left at the intersection. The trail to the right will be your return route.

1.0 The trail ends at an overlook of a salt meadow with Brave Boat Harbor in the background. To complete the hike, return the way you came.

1.5 Bear left at the intersection.

1.8 Pass the Cross Trail.

2.1 Arrive back at the trailhead.

2 Vaughan Woods

Several miles of trails crisscross mature pine woods and meander along the tidal Salmon Falls River. The hike follows an old bridle path through the woods to the southern end of the park, passing the Warren homesite. You return to the trailhead along the river, where there are several overlooks.

Start: Marked trailhead in picnic area at east end of parking lot

Distance: 2-mile loop

Approximate hiking time: 2–3 hours

Difficulty: Easy

Best season: Vaughan Woods Memorial State Park is open Memorial Day to Labor Day. You can easily walk into the park when the gate is closed during the off-season.

Trail surface: Woodland path

Land status: Vaughan Woods Memorial State Park

Nearest town: South Berwick

Other users: None

Water availability: Spigot near trailhead

Canine compatibility: Dogs must be on a 4-foot leash at all times.

Fees and permits: Park entrance fee, payable at self-service kiosk

Maps: *DeLorme: Maine Atlas & Gazetteer* map 1; USGS Dover East

Trail contact: Vaughan Woods Memorial State Park, (207) 490-4079, www.maine.gov/doc/parks

Finding the trailhead: From exit 7 on the Maine Turnpike (I-95), drive 0.4 mile to US 1. Turn right and drive 0.7 mile south on US 1. Turn right onto ME 91 and drive 7.6 miles to the junction with ME 236. Go straight across ME 236 onto Old South Road and drive 1.1 miles. Turn left onto Oldfields Road and drive 0.4 mile. The park entrance is on the right. Drive to the far end of the parking area. The trailhead is in the picnic area at the end of the parking lot. GPS: N43 12.721' / W70 48.752'

The Hike

The hike begins in a piney picnic grove. The field that you drove through to get to the trailhead is more typical of this land's historical character. Before the first European settlers, Native Americans kept open areas for farming and berrying along the Salmon Falls River. They rotated land about every ten years, leaving a patchwork of farmland, brambles, new forest, and mature forest. Later, when the Hamilton family built their house overlooking the river, almost none of the land that is now the state park was forested.

As you follow the Bridle Path through mature softwood forest, it is hard to believe it is relatively young. Just before the trail turns toward the river, you pass the Warren home-site. James Warren built a cabin here around 1656. Just to the west of the cellar hole is the family cemetery. All that remains are several tilted stones whose inscriptions have long been worn off.

The Bridle Path ends at the Salmon Falls River. Here is the first of several overlooks with benches that you will pass along the River Run. The river here is tidal. In colonial times ships could navigate all the way to the falls in South Berwick to deliver supplies and pick up loads of lumber.

Cow Cove is reputed to be where one of those ships delivered the area's first cow in the 1630s. Beyond White Oak Point, the hillside becomes steeper. The trail follows a bluff overlooking the river through rusty needles beneath mature trees. Herons and sometimes egrets hunt in the shallow river, while ducks and geese bob on the water.

The trail descends again to the river at Hamilton House View. From the shore you can look across a pond-like inlet to the restored mansion set back from the river on a grassy

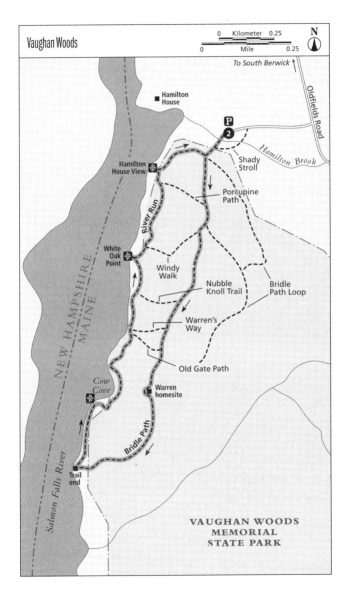

Vaughan Woods

0   Kilometer   0.25

0   Mile   0.25

N

To South Berwick

Oldfields Road

Hamilton House

P
2

Hamilton Brook

Shady Stroll

Hamilton House View

Porcupine Path

River Run

White Oak Point

Windy Walk

Nubble Knoll Trail

Bridle Path Loop

Warren's Way

Old Gate Path

NEW HAMPSHIRE

MAINE

Cow Cove

Warren homesite

Bridle Path

Salmon Falls River

Trail end

VAUGHAN WOODS
MEMORIAL
STATE PARK

knoll. Just before River Run ends at the Bridle Path, a side trail leads to the house, which is open to visitors in season. The house was restored around the turn of the last century by the Vaughan family, who bought the property at the urging of Maine author Sarah Orne Jewett. The Vaughans donated to the state the land that is now Vaughan Woods Memorial State Park.

Miles and Directions

0.0 Start from the trail sign in the picnic area at the east end of the parking lot. Descend 140 feet, passing Shady Stroll. Across Hamilton Brook, bear left onto the Bridle Path.

0.1 Pass the Bridle Path Loop.

0.2 Pass the Porcupine Path and then the other end of the Bridle Path Loop.

0.3 Pass Windy Walk.

0.4 Pass Nubble Knoll Trail.

0.5 Pass Warren's Way, then in another 200 feet pass Old Gate Path

0.6 Pass the Warren homesite.

0.9 The Bridle Trail ends at the River Run at an overlook of the Salmon Falls River. Turn right onto River Run.

1.1 Arrive at Cow Cove.

1.3 Pass Old Gate Path, then Warren's Way.

1.4 Pass Nubble Knoll Trail.

1.5 Reach White Oak Point.

1.6 Pass Windy Walk.

1.7 Pass Porcupine Path.

1.8 Reach Hamilton House View.

1.9 River Run turns east away from the river and passes the trail to Hamilton House. Continue straight ahead to the Bridle Path. Bear left onto the Bridle Path.

2.0 Arrive back at the trailhead.

3 Mount Agamenticus

Mount Agamenticus is popular with hikers and sightseers. The hike begins at the summit and descends northwest, tracking an abandoned ski run into a quiet valley, then returns over partially open Second Hill. This hike visits most of the habitats around Mount Agamenticus while avoiding most of the crowded trails.

Start: Kiosk north of parking area on summit

Distance: 4-mile double loop

Approximate hiking time: 3–4 hours

Difficulty: More challenging

Best season: May–Oct

Trail surface: Woodland path

Land status: Mount Agamenticus Conservation Region

Nearest towns: York and Ogunqui

Other users: Cedar Trail open to snowmobiles and ATVs; some trails open to bikes

Water availability: Summit Lodge

Canine compatibility: Dogs must be on a leash at all times.

Fees and permits: None

Maps: *DeLorme: Maine Atlas & Gazetteer* map 1; USGS York Harbor

Trail contact: Mount Agamenticus Conservation Region, (207) 361-1102, www.agamenticus.org

Finding the trailhead: From exit 19 on the Maine Turnpike (I-95), take ME 9 east toward Wells and drive 1.5 miles to US 1. Turn right onto US 1 and drive 5.2 miles into Ogunquit. Turn right onto Clay Hill Road and drive 4 miles to a T-intersection. Turn right onto Mountain Road and drive 1.6 miles. Turn right onto Summit Road at the Mount Agamenticus sign and drive 0.6 mile to the summit. Turn right into the parking area. The trailhead is at the kiosk north of the parking area. GPS: N43 13.385' / W70 41.539'

The Hike

Mount Agamenticus is the highest point in York County. It was an important landmark for sailors along the otherwise featureless Southern Coast. The mountain is a granite pluton that was laid down about 200 million years ago. It is related to the White Mountains, not Maine's other various granite features like Mount Desert Island and Katahdin—which are hundreds of millions of years older than Mount Agamenticus.

The hike begins on the summit, which is busy with the converted ski lodge, lookout towers, and communications towers. The views from the summit reach from the White Mountains in the west to the bright white of York County's beaches.

Across the grassy summit, descend on the Sweet Fern Trail away from the crowds and down into quiet forest over bare granite slabs. The hike continues descending down the Goosefoot Trail through mature hardwoods. The Goosefoot Trail ends at the Cedar Trail, a multiuse trail that winds through the woods past low swampy areas.

Follow the Porcupine Trail from the valley onto Second Hill. The Ridge Trail winds along the hill through semi-open oak forest to the summit. You get glimpses through the trees of Mount Agamenticus in the distance. The pale granite face of Vulture's View shines in the sun.

As you hike back to the mountain and climb the Vulture's View Trail, look for scratches on the bedrock left by rocks scraped across the granite by moving glaciers. Once back on the summit, make a circuit around to all of the various overlooks and viewing platforms.

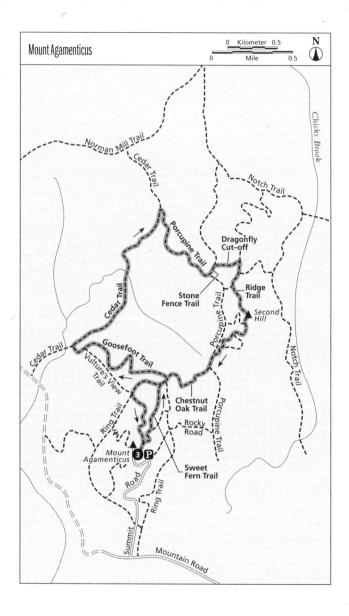

Mount Agamenticus

Norman Mill Trail

Cedar Trail

Notch Trail

Chicks Brook

Porcupine Trail

Dragonfly Cut-off

Stone Fence Trail

Ridge Trail

Cedar Trail

Porcupine Trail

Second Hill

Cedar Trail

Goosefoot Trail

Vulture's View Trail

Ring Trail

Chestnut Oak Trail

Porcupine Trail

Rocky Road

Notch Trail

Mount Agamenticus

3 P

Sweet Fern Trail

Ring Trail

Road

Summit

Ring Trail

Mountain Road

0   Kilometer   0.5

0   Mile   0.5

N

Miles and Directions

0.0 Start from the kiosk north of the summit parking lot. Cross the grassy summit, heading northeast past the Summit Lodge. Descend off the summit on the Sweet Fern Trail.

0.1 Pass Vulture's View Trail.

0.3 Turn right onto Ring Trail.

0.4 Turn left onto Goosefoot Trail.

1.0 Continue past Vulture's View Trail.

1.1 Turn right onto Cedar Trail.

1.9 Turn right onto Porcupine Trail.

2.3 Turn left onto Stone Fence Trail.

2.4 Turn right onto a cross trail.

2.5 Turn right onto Ridge Trail.

2.6 Pass Incline Trail on the left then another cross trail on the right. Continue on Ridge Trail toward Second Hill.

2.8 Cross the summit of Second Hill.

3.1 Descend off Second Hill on Ridge Trail. Turn left onto Porcupine Trail.

3.2 Turn right onto Chestnut Oak Trail.

3.5 Arrive back at Ring Trail. Go straight onto Ring Trail.

3.7 Turn left onto Vulture's View Trail.

4.0 Arrive back at the summit and trailhead.

4 Kennebunk Plains

The trails around the Kennebunk Plains are mostly abandoned sand roads left from when the plain was a commercial blueberry operation. The hike follows around the outside of the plains, skirting the woods and following Cold Water Brook and then the Mousam River. The plains are filled with blueberries and northern blazing star—an endangered wildflower found nowhere else is such numbers.

Start: Trailhead at west end of parking area on north side of ME 99

Distance: 1.9-mile loop

Approximate hiking time: 1 hour

Difficulty: Easy

Best season: Late summer, when the blueberries are ripe and the northern blazing stars are in bloom

Trail surface: Sandy woods roads

Land status: Kennebunk Plains Wildlife Management Area

Nearest town: Kennebunk

Other users: Bikes allowed on trails

Water availability: None

Canine compatibility: Dogs must be under control at all times.

Fees and permits: None

Maps: *DeLorme: Maine Atlas & Gazetteer* map 2; USGS Kennebunk

Trail contact: Kennebunk Land Trust, (207) 985-8734, www .kennebunklandtrust.org/ preserves/kcnnebunk-wildlife -management-area.php

Finding the trailhead: From exit 25 on the Maine Turnpike (I-95), drive west on Alfred Road toward West Kennebunk. Drive 1 mile to a stop sign at Mill Street; there is a sign to ME 99 at the intersection. Turn left onto Mill Street, which crosses the Mousam River after 0.5 mile. Up the hill across the river, turn right onto ME 99 (0.7 mile from Alfred Road). Drive 1.1 miles west on ME 99. There are parking areas for the preserve on both sides of the road. The trailhead is at the west end of the parking area north of ME 99. There are no signs for the preserve. GPS: N43 24.144' / W70 37.509'

The Hike

The grasslands of the Kennebunk Plains are among the rarest and most endangered habitat type in Maine and New England. The plain was formed about 14,000 years ago when streams flowing out of the receding glaciers sorted the sands and gravels, leaving a landscape that won't support trees and is subject to frequent droughts and fires. The plain is essentially a coastal ecosystem. As the glaciers of the last ice age melted, ocean levels rose. Because the land had been depressed by the weight of the ice sitting on it, the shore was miles inland from where it is today. As the land rebounded, the coast retreated to where it is today, leaving ecosystems like the Kennebunk Plains up and down the southern Maine coast.

For a time the Kennebunk Plains was used as a commercial blueberry barren. Enough blueberry bushes survive to make a late summer hike a snacking opportunity. Today the Kennebunk Plains is a Nature Conservancy preserve and a state wildlife management area.

The highlight of the plains is the northern blazing star, an endangered wildflower that turns the plains purple in August. The Kennebunk Plains supports the only population of northern blazing star in Maine and the largest concentration of the wildflower anywhere in the world.

On the hike you may see a number of other rare plants and animals, as well as numerous songbirds and butterflies. The trails through and around the Kennebunk Plains are

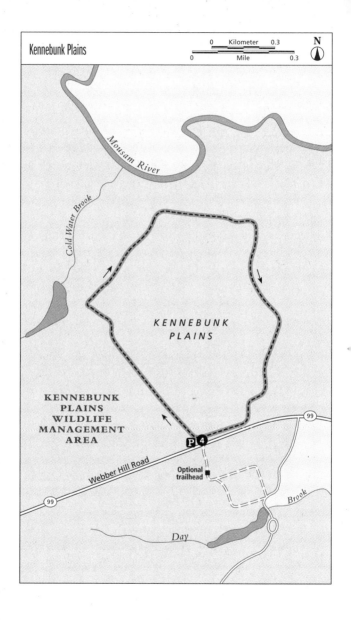

Kennebunk Plains

KENNEBUNK
PLAINS

KENNEBUNK
PLAINS
WILDLIFE
MANAGEMENT
AREA

Mousam River

Cold Water Brook

Webber Hill Road

Optional
trailhead

Brook

Day

99

99

N

0   Kilometer   0.3

0   Mile   0.3

mostly what remains of the roads used by blueberry farmers. They are unmarked but easy to follow.

There are more trails on the south side of ME 99, across from the trailhead. The trails on the south side of the road are also unmarked and extend into the woods, where there is a small pond.

Miles and Directions

0.0 Start from the trailhead at the west end of the parking area on the north side of ME 99.

0.2 Pass a trail that leads west.

0.4 Turn left toward Cold Water Brook.

0.5 The trail bends to the north, along the stream.

0.6 Continue straight ahead on the main trail.

1.1 The trail turns south at the edge of the woods. An unmaintained trail leads north to the Mousam River.

1.4 The trail bends to the right.

1.6 Cross a trail that leads west across the plains.

1.9 Arrive back at the trailhead.

5 Carson Trail

The Carson Trail is a self-guided nature trail that follows the Merriland River and Branch Brook. Along the way you get fine views of the extensive salt marsh along the Little River. Many shore and wading birds can be seen here. What birds are where changes as the land floods twice a day on the rising tide. The trail winds along the edge of the salt marsh in a forest of mature white pines and hemlocks. In late spring, look for lady slippers in the woods.

Start: Carson Trailhead at south end of parking area
Distance: 1.3-mile lollipop
Approximate hiking time: 1–2 hours
Difficulty: Easy
Best season: Apr–Oct
Trail surface: Graded woodland path
Land status: Rachel Carson National Wildlife Refuge
Nearest town: Wells

Other users: None
Water availability: None
Canine compatibility: Dogs must be on a leash at all times.
Fees and permits: None
Maps: *DeLorme: Maine Atlas & Gazetteer* map 3; USGS Wells
Trail contact: Rachel Carson National Wildlife Refuge, (207) 646-9226, www.fws.gov/refuge/rachel_carson

Finding the trailhead: From exit 19 on I-95, drive east on ME 9 for 1.6 miles to US 1 in Wells. Turn left on US 1, heading north. Drive 1.9 miles to Port Road (ME 9). Turn right onto Port Road; there is a sign for the Rachel Carson National Wildlife Refuge. Do not follow the NWR signs to the Laudholm Division. Drive 0.7 mile to the refuge entrance and turn right into the refuge parking area at the large sign. The trailhead is at the south end of the parking area, at the information kiosk. GPS: N43 20.831' / W70 32.898'

The Hike

Kennebunk is at the heart of an arc of the Maine coast made up of sandy beaches, salt marshes, and prominent rounded heads. Between Kittery and Cape Elizabeth, many of the marshes are protected as part of the Rachel Carson National Wildlife Refuge. In Wells, at the refuge's headquarters, is the Carson Trail. This short, easy hike loops along the Merriland River and Branch Brook, with views of the surrounding salt marshes and islands of forest. The path is a self-guided nature trail that explains the importance of salt marsh habitat and the plants and animals that live there.

There are a number of overlooks along the trail. The views from them change dramatically as the tide ebbs and flows. At low tide the stream channels are low, mud-lined snakes winding through the salt grasses. You can find wading birds feeding there. Often families of ducks paddle along the channels, feeding. In the salt grass are ponds that are higher than the streams; water is isolated in bowls until the tide comes in and the water rises to them. These pools attract herons and snowy egrets. The southern Maine shores are the farthest north these egrets can be found along the Atlantic Coast.

The southernmost point on the hike is where the Merriland River and Branch Brook flow together to form the Little River. It really is a little river. From the overlook it is less than 0.5 mile to where the river empties into the ocean. You can see the river's mouth across the waving salt grass. Obviously, the river's course is about as indirect as it can be, making the water's journey to the ocean nearly three times as long as it needs to be. Out across the expanse of salt marsh between the trail and Crescent Surf Beach, clouds of snowy egrets move back and forth—seemingly at random. It's not

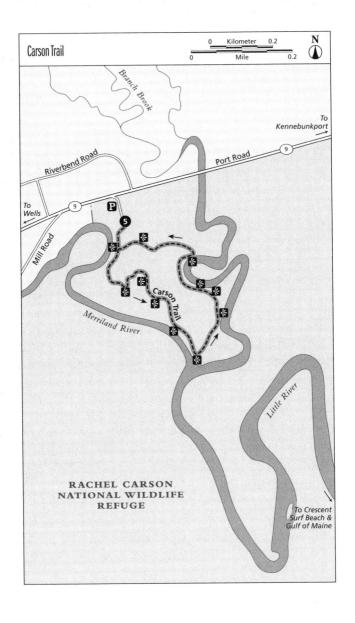

unusual to see ospreys and eagles soaring above the salt marsh or winging with purpose to or from their nest.

If you spend all your time looking out across the salt marsh, you'll miss the beauty of the woods the trail passes through. The forest is mature evergreens, mostly white pine and hemlock. In late spring and early summer, look for lady slipper orchids and other wildflowers.

After completing the hike, you may want to visit one of the area's beaches. Try nearby Parsons Beach. To get there, drive east on ME 9 for 1.4 miles and turn right onto Parsons Beach Road. Beach access is at the end of the road. You can swim and play on the beach, as well as explore the mouth of the Mousam River. Much of the lower Mousam River is part of the wildlife refuge. From the mouth of the river, you get to see a salt marsh from the other side.

Miles and Directions

0.0 Start from the information kiosk at the south end of the parking area.

0.1 Stay right at the fork.

0.2 The trail follows along the Merriland River to the first overlook.

0.6 The trail follows the Merriland River to an overlook at the confluence with Branch Brook. From here the combined stream, Little River, meanders to the ocean through a salt marsh.

0.7 The trail follows Branch Brook to an overlook of an extensive salt marsh.

1.0 The trail continues following Branch Brook, passing two overlooks, before turning inland.

1.2 Arrive back at the fork in the trail. Turn right to return to the trailhead.

1.3 Arrive back at the trailhead.

6 Timber Point

Timber Point is nearly an island. It is separated from Goose Rocks Beach by the Little River. The trail follows a lane through an open forest of mostly oak to the rocky point. At low tide you can cross to Timber Island. There are no trails on the island, but you can wander its small wooded center or explore the jumbled rocks along the shore. There is access from the trailhead to the Little River and a white sand beach in Curtis Cove.

Start: Trailhead next to information sign at south end of parking area
Distance: 1.9 miles out and back
Approximate hiking time: 1–2 hours
Difficulty: Easy
Best season: May–Oct
Trail surface: Gravel lane and woodland path
Land status: Rachel Carson National Wildlife Refuge

Nearest town: Biddeford
Other users: None
Water availability: None
Canine compatibility: Dogs must be on a leash at all times.
Fees and permits: None
Maps: *DeLorme: Maine Atlas & Gazetteer* map 3; USGS Biddeford
Trail contact: Rachel Carson National Wildlife Refuge, (207) 646-9226, www.fws.gov/refuge/rachel_carson

Finding the trailhead: From exit 36 on I-95 in Saco, drive south on I-195 for 1 mile. Exit at Industrial Park Road. Turn left at the light onto Industrial Park Road and drive 0.6 mile. Turn left onto ME 112 and drive 1.2 miles into Saco. Turn right onto ME 9 south and drive 7.7 miles through Saco and Biddeford. Turn left onto Granite Point Road and drive 1.6 miles to the end of the road. Parking is on the right; the trailhead is straight ahead. GPS: N43 24.436' / W70 23.730'

The Hike

Timber Point and Timber Island are part of the Rachel Carson National Wildlife Refuge. The salt marsh along the Little River that you follow to get to the trailhead is part of the refuge as well. You are likely to see wading birds, ducks, and seabirds on your way to the trailhead and along the hike.

Timber Point is nearly an island, a roundish chunk of granite at the mouth of the Little River. The hike follows a lane along the river through an open oak forest. The point itself is a rough lawn with a line of twisty oaks along the rocky shore.

Across the river mouth is Goose Rocks Beach. You stand on rocky ground surrounded by nature, while a short distance away is a wide sand beach busy with people. Behind the beach crowd boxy houses. It's quite a contrast.

Most of the land you drove through to get to the hike and the Goose Rocks Beach area were burned in the great fire of 1947. After the fire Goose Rocks Beach was an ash black landscape of crumbing chimneys and a few skeletal trees. Farther north along the coast, Fortune's Rocks also burned. But Timber Point didn't.

From the point you can see the surviving mansion that overlooks the shore. In 2011, when Timber Point became part of the wildlife refuge, the house became the Timber Point Center.

At low tide you can cross to trail-less Timber Island and explore its rocky shore and wooded interior. Be sure to check the tide chart posted on Timber Point before crossing or you could be stranded on the island.

Before heading back to your car, take time to explore the rocky channel between the point and Timber Island. At the

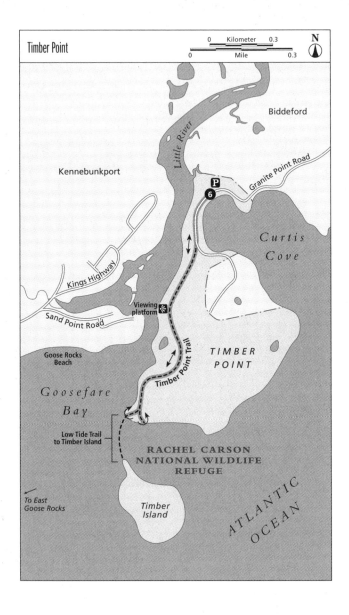

Timber Point

0 Kilometer 0.3
0 Mile 0.3

N

Biddeford

Little River

Kennebunkport

Granite Point Road

P
6

Curtis Cove

Kings Highway

Viewing platform

Sand Point Road

Goose Rocks Beach

TIMBER POINT

Timber Point Trail

Goosefare Bay

Low Tide Trail to Timber Island

RACHEL CARSON NATIONAL WILDLIFE REFUGE

To East Goose Rocks

Timber Island

ATLANTIC OCEAN

trailhead you can explore the Little River and its salt marsh or swim in Curtis Cove.

Miles and Directions

0.0 From the parking area, follow the lane south between Curtis Cove and the Little River.

0.3 A side trail leads 100 feet to a viewing platform along the Little River, with a view across the river of Goose Rocks Beach.

0.8 Arrive at Timber Point. *Option:* If the tide dial gives you the green light, you can cross the narrow channel to Timber Island. There are no trails on the island.

0.9 The trail loops around Timber Point, with several access points to the rocky shoreline. To complete the hike, return the way you came.

1.9 Arrive back at the trailhead.

7 Saco Heath

The Saco Heath Trail winds through increasingly wet forest before emerging onto the heath. The boardwalk crosses open heath, dotted with scrub pines, to a slight height of land that supports a forest. This is the southernmost peat bog in Maine. Along the boardwalk you can find northern bog species as well as more southern species, making it a unique ecosystem.

Start: Trailhead next to information kiosk at north end of parking area
Distance: 2.2 miles out and back
Approximate hiking time: 1–2 hours
Difficulty: Easy
Best season: May–Oct
Trail surface: Woodland path and boardwalk
Land status: Saco Heath Preserve

Nearest town: Saco
Other users: None
Water availability: None
Canine compatibility: Dogs are not permitted in the preserve.
Fees and permits: None
Maps: *DeLorme: Maine Atlas & Gazetteer* map 3; USGS Old Orchard Beach
Trail contact: The Nature Conservancy, www.nature.org/our initiatives/regions/northamerica/unitedstates/maine

Finding the trailhead: From exit 36 on I-95 in Saco, drive south on I-195 for 1 mile. Exit at Industrial Park Road. Turn left at the light onto Industrial Park Road and drive 0.6 mile. Turn right onto ME 112 and drive 2.2 miles. The trailhead parking is on the right at the sign for Saco Heath Preserve. The trailhead is at the north end of the parking lot. GPS: N43 32.486' / W70 28.885'

The Hike

Saco Heath is the farthest south raised peat bog in Maine. It was formed about 9,000 years ago after the glaciers retreated. The heath formed when two acidic lakes became choked with partially decomposed plant material. Over time a dome of sphagnum moss grew over the water. Today, in places, there is 20 feet of saturated peat and moss beneath the boardwalk.

The 1,223-acre preserve protects most of Saco Heath. The hike only give you a hint of its extent. As you hike to the boardwalk, notice how the ground becomes increasingly wet. The trees growing there change, as does the understory. Early in the hike look for trillium and other acid-tolerant forest species. As you near the open heath, look for blueberries and huckleberries. On the heath itself you can find pitcher plants, orchids, cotton grass, several kinds of laurels, and cranberries. Scrub pines grow in loose stands like something from a Dr. Seuss book. Fingers of evergreen forest grow on higher ground in the heath.

Because Saco Heath is so far south, both northern and southern species can be found here. For example, the heath is about as far north as you'll find the endangered Atlantic white cedar.

In May the heath is awash with the purple blooms of the laurel. Most of the heath's residents aren't as showy. You need to take your time and examine the bog—even get down on your hands and knees and peer at the growth beside the boardwalk. Tiny plants and flowers are there for you to find if you take the time.

Without the boardwalk you would sink into the springy moss, soaking your feet and calves. Travel across the bog is

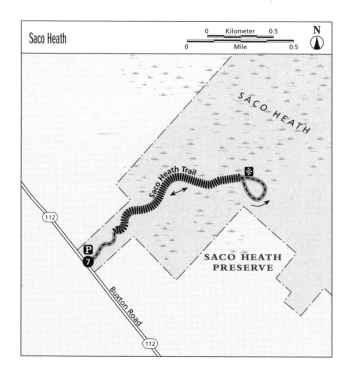

almost impossible without the boardwalk—not to mention the damage you would do, leaving deep impressions in the bog that would persist for years. So, take your time and appreciate the gift of access to this unique ecosystem the boardwalk offers you.

Miles and Directions

0.0 The Saco Heath Trail begins at the north end of the parking area, next to the information kiosk.

0.2 The trail wanders through a piney woods to the beginning of the boardwalk. Where the boardwalk breaks out of the woods and onto the heath, there is a bench.

0.9 The boardwalk ends where the trail reaches a pine woods. Turn right onto the loop trail.

1.2 A side trail leads 100 feet to an overlook of Saco Heath.

1.3 Arrive back at the boardwalk. Turn right to complete the hike.

2.2 Arrive back at the trailhead.

8 Douglas Mountain

Douglas Mountain is the highest of the Saddleback Hills between the Saco River and Sebago Lake. The stone tower on its summit offers fine views of nearby Sebago Lake, the White Mountains, and the Maine coast. The trail climbs steadily from a damp hardwood forest to the rocky summit, then descends steeply down exposed bedrock to Douglas Mountain Road.

Start: Douglas Mountain Trailhead at east end of parking area
Distance: 2.2-mile loop
Approximate hiking time: 2 hours
Difficulty: More challenging
Best season: May–Oct
Trail surface: Woodland path
Land status: Douglas Mountain Preserve
Nearest town: Standish

Other users: The last section of the hike is a road walk.
Water availability: None
Canine compatibility: Dogs must be under control at all times.
Fees and permits: None
Maps: *DeLorme: Maine Atlas & Gazetteer* map 4; USGS North Sebago and Steep Falls
Trail contact: Town of Sebago, (207) 787-2457, www.townof sebago.org/Pages/visiting

Finding the trailhead: From exit 48 on the Maine Turnpike (I-95), follow ME 25 west 6.8 miles to downtown Gorham. Continue west on ME 25 for 2.9 miles. Turn right onto ME 113 and drive 7 miles. Turn right onto ME 11/107 and drive north 1.8 miles. Stay straight on ME 107 and drive 3.8 miles. Turn left onto Dyke Mountain Road at the sign for Douglas Mountain and drive 0.9 mile. Turn left onto Douglas Mountain Road and drive 0.2 mile. Turn left onto Douglas Mountain Preserve Road at the sign and drive 0.1 mile to the parking area. The trailhead is at the east end of the parking area. GPS: N43 52.648' / W70 41.577'

The Hike

The Eagle Scout Trail wanders through a hardwood forest, crossing and sometimes following an ATV trail. There is little underbrush beneath the tall hardwoods, their canopies woven together, blocking out much of the light.

The trail leaves the wide multiuse trail and begins a short rocky climb up out of the hardwoods into a mixed forest. Dappled sunlight allows for a busy understory of shrubs, moss, lichen, and herbaceous plants. As you follow the Nature Loop Trail south, partial views open up to the east—hints of what you'll see from the summit.

On the semi-open summit is a 16-foot stone observation tower built in 1925 by William Blackman, the then-owner of the mountain. Harry Douglas, whose family the mountain was named for, used his team of oxen to haul to the summit the stones, mortar, and water needed to build the tower.

A staircase winds up the inside of the tower to the top. You have fine views in every direction. To the west the White Mountains are a jagged line on the horizon beyond a series of forested hills. To the north the flat coastal plain gives way to hills and mountains. And to the east, across the blue expanse of Sebago Lake, lies the coast with its white sand beaches and dark waters. A sign on the tower shows you what you are seeing, putting names to the various mountains and lakes.

From the summit the Ledges Trail drops steeply down a series of bedrock ledges to Douglas Mountain Road. Follow the road downhill to the trailhead. As you stroll down the road, you have fine views north and west across sloping hay meadows.

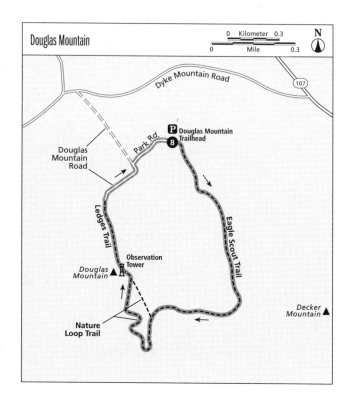

Miles and Directions

0.0 Start from the Douglas Mountain Trailhead at the east end
of the parking area. Follow the well-blazed Eagle Scout Trail
mostly along an ATV trail.

0.7 At a marked intersection, the Eagle Scout Trail leaves the ATV
trail and begins to climb.

1.0 Turn left onto the Nature Loop Trail.

1.1 The trail crosses ledges with views east.

1.5 Arrive at the summit of Douglas Mountain. To complete the hike, descend from the summit on the Ledges Trail.

1.8 The Ledges Trail ends at Douglas Mountain Road. Turn right onto the road.

2.1 Turn right onto the park road.

2.2 Arrive back at the trailhead.

9 Mount Cutler

The hike on Mount Cutler may be the best mountain hike in Maine that doesn't reach the summit. The trail climbs steeply up the mountain's east face, with fine views of the Saco River valley. Once on the ridge there are several overlooks with expansive views. From the notch you can bushwhack to the actual summit of Mount Cutler.

Start: Sign on far side of railroad tracks south of parking area
Distance: 3-mile loop
Approximate hiking time: 3-4 hours
Difficulty: Most challenging
Best season: May–Oct
Trail surface: Woodland path
Land status: Private property with trails maintained by the Appalachian Mountain Club
Nearest town: Hiram
Other users: None
Water availability: None
Canine compatibility: Parts of the hike are too steep for dogs.
Fees and permits: None
Maps: *DeLorme: Maine Atlas & Gazetteer* map 4; USGS Hiram and Cornish
Trail contact: None

Finding the trailhead: From exit 48 on the Maine Turnpike (I-95), follow ME 25 west 6.8 miles to downtown Gorham. Continue west on ME 25 for 2.9 miles. Turn right onto ME 113 and drive 17 miles into Hiram. Just across the bridge over the Saco River, turn left onto River Road. Drive 250 feet, then turn right onto Mount View Avenue and drive 0.1 mile. Turn right into the parking area along the railroad tracks. The trailhead is to the south on the other side of the train tracks. GPS: N43 52.610' / W70 48.317'

The Hike

Mount Cutler is one of the mountains west of Hiram known as Sunday's Rocks. Mount Misery and Peaked Mountain are both higher, but untrailed. According to Captain Henry Young Brown—for whom nearby Brownfield was named in 1791—the name Sunday's Rocks appeared on a map he had seen. The mountains were named for an Abenaki sagamore who supposedly fell to his death from the cliffs on Mount Cutler.

The hike first passes through a grove of mature white pines, passing a short side trail to an abandoned gold mine. The Barnes Trail climbs up a narrow rock-filled gulley then angles up a steep rock face. As you climb, fine views of Hiram and the Saco River valley emerge.

The trail climbs across a subsidiary peak of Mount Cutler, connected to the main mountain by a long, narrow ridge. The precipitous south face of the mountain offers expansive views of the Saco River valley and the distant coast. Here and there views to the west and north open up: One moment you can see the White Mountains crenelated against the blue sky, the next Pleasant Mountain rising among green hills.

The trail drops into The Notch. To the west rises the wooded summit of Mount Cutler. No trail leads there, but it is fairly easy to bushwhack up the slope to the summit if you want to. From The Notch the Saco Ridge Trail slabs eastward around the mountain, then drops steeply into the Saco River valley. Most of the hike is through hardwood forests that abound in wildflowers in the spring before the trees leaf out.

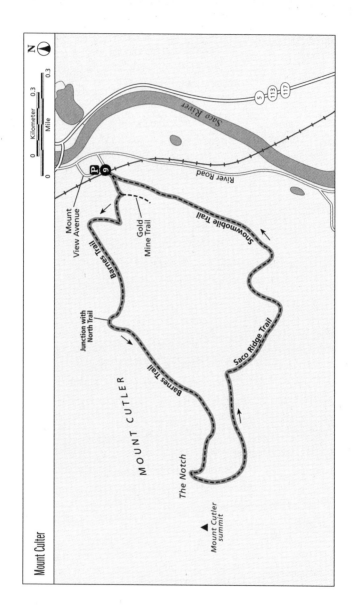

Mount Culter

Miles and Directions

0.0 Start from the trailhead at the brown information sign 100 feet south of the parking area across the railroad tracks. Two hundred feet up the trail, turn right onto the Barnes Trail.

0.1 Bear right, staying on the Barnes Trail. The trail to the left leads 300 feet to the site of an abandoned gold mine.

0.7 The Barnes Trail climbs steeply up a rocky slope, with fine views of Hiram and the Saco River valley. Pass the North Trail on the right.

1.2 The trail climbs gently across a semi-open ridge with occasional fine views.

1.3 Descend into The Notch. To the west is the untrailed summit of Mount Cutler. You can easily bushwhack up the slope. In The Notch the trail changes names to the Saco Ridge Trail.

2.2 Bear left, staying on the Saco Ridge Trail.

2.4 Descend, steeply at times, to the end of the Saco Ridge Trail. Turn left on the Snowmobile Trail.

2.7 Bear left, staying on the Snowmobile Trail.

2.9 Arrive back at the Barnes Trail. Continue straight ahead to complete the hike.

3.0 Arrive back at the trailhead.

10 Burnt Meadow Mountain

Burnt Meadow Mountain is a long mountain running roughly north–south, with several peaks in Brownfield. The hike leads to North Peak, with an option to climb Stone Mountain. Both peaks and especially the approach to North Peak offer fine views in every direction. This is the most challenging hike in this guide, but well worth the effort.

Start: Burnt Meadow Mountain Trailhead at northeast corner of parking area

Distance: 3.7-mile lollipop

Approximate hiking time: 3–4 hours

Difficulty: Most challenging

Best season: May–Oct

Trail surface: Woodland path

Land status: Private property with trails maintained by the Friends of Burnt Meadow Mountain

Nearest town: Brownfield

Other users: None

Water availability: None

Canine compatibility: Dogs must be under control at all times.

Fees and permits: None

Maps: *DeLorme: Maine Atlas & Gazetteer* map 4; USGS Brownfield

Trail contact: Friends of Burnt Meadow Mountain, www.friends ofburntmeadowmountains.com

Finding the trailhead: From exit 48 on the Maine Turnpike (I-95), follow ME 25 west 6.8 miles to downtown Gorham. Continue west on ME 25 for 2.9 miles. Turn right onto ME 113 and drive 23.5 miles to ME 160. Turn left onto ME 160 and drive south 3.2 miles. The trailhead parking is on the right at the sign. The trailhead is at the northeast corner of the parking area. GPS: N43 55.094' / W70 52.990'

The Hike

Burnt Meadow Mountain rises just south of the town of Brownfield. It runs roughly north–south, with three separate peaks. The mountain—and the pond at its feet—were named for a nearby fire in colonial times. The original trail up North Peak was obliterated in the 1947 fire that destroyed most of the buildings in Brownfield. What had been a thriving farming community with several mansions and the usual municipal and commercial buildings was reduced to ashes. Seventy-five percent of the town's taxable property burned.

The fire, one of several that burned in Maine that week in October, swept down from Fryeburg and burned more than 21,000 acres before it was contained. The wind-driven fire burned with such heat and intensity that even the topsoil beneath the trees burned.

The hike climbs a rocky ridge to a semi-open shoulder of Burnt Meadow Mountain with some views. Beyond the fork in the trail, the Burnt Meadow Trail drops into a deeply wooded saddle, then begins to climb in earnest. As you climb, views open in every direction, distracting you from the steepness of the climb.

In contrast, the views are somewhat limited from North Peak. As you descend on the Twin Brook Trail, you have intermittent views west of the White Mountains—Burnt Meadow Mountain is only a few miles from the New Hampshire border.

The trail descends into the deep valley between North Peak and Stone Mountain—the highest of Burnt Meadow Mountain's summits. The mature hardwoods are mostly the same age, a result of the 1947 fire. What surrounds you is the forest that sprang up after that disaster.

Burnt Meadow Mountain

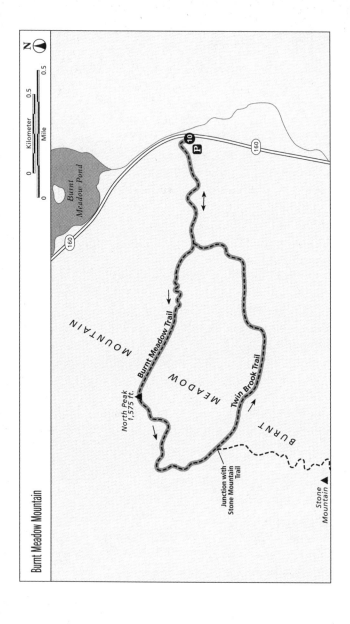

Miles and Directions

0.0 Start from the trailhead at the northeast corner of the parking area.

0.5 The Burnt Meadow Trail climbs over bare rock with some views to a junction with the Twin Brook Trail. Bear right, staying on Burnt Meadow Trail.

1.3 The trail climbs steeply, with fine views to the summit of North Peak.

2.0 Descend off North Peak on the Twin Brook Trail into the notch between North Peak and Stone Mountain. Pass the Stone Mountain Trail. *Option:* The Stone Mountain Trail climbs to the summit of Stone Mountain—the highest of Burnt Meadow Mountain's several peak—in 0.7 mile.

3.2 Arrive back at the Burnt Meadow Trail. Turn right to return to the trailhead.

3.7 Arrive back at the trailhead.

11 Two Lights State Park

This hike is an easy ramble around the perimeter of Two Lights State Park. You pass the remnants of a World War II gun emplacement and a rocky shoreline of broken shale. The bedrock here is parallel to the coast, creating a very different headland than any to the north.

Start: Information signs south of parking area in front of bunker
Distance: 1.2-mile loop
Approximate hiking time: 1 hour
Difficulty: Easy
Best season: May–Oct
Trail surface: Woodland path and graded trail
Land status: Two Lights State Park
Nearest town: Cape Elizabeth
Other users: None

Water availability: None
Canine compatibility: Dogs must be on a 4-foot leash at all times.
Fees and permits: Park entrance fee
Maps: *DeLorme: Maine Atlas & Gazetteer* map 3; USGS Cape Elizabeth
Trail contact: Two Lights State Park, (207) 799-5871, www .maine.gov/twolights

Finding the trailhead: From exit 2 on I-295 in South Portland, drive south on the Scarborough Connector 2.1 miles to US 1. Drive south on US 1 for 0.8 mile. Turn left onto ME 207 at the first light and drive 2.9 miles. Turn left onto ME 77 and drive 5.7 miles. Turn right onto Two Lights Road and drive 1.1 miles. Turn right onto Tower Drive at the Two Lights State Park sign. Parking is at the end of the road beyond the entrance gate. The trailhead is at the information signs south of the parking area. GPS: N43 33.597' / W70 12.300'

The Hike

The first things you are likely to notice in Two Lights State Park are the grass-covered bunker along the shore and the cylindrical tower on a rise inland. Both are remains of a World War II gun emplacement built to help protect Portland. The war ended before the gun emplacement was finished. The bunker housed the command center, and the tower was an observation post where soldiers would have scanned the Gulf of Maine for enemy ships and submarines. The guns themselves sat on the flat areas on either side of the bunker.

As you hike through the woods and then along the shore, you are likely to notice that there are no lighthouses in the park—or even visible from it. The two lighthouses that gave the park its name were farther east at the end of Two Lights Road. Only one still exists, the Cape Elizabeth Light, which sits high on a hill above Dyer Cove.

The bedrock in the park is folded and deformed mudstone, known to geologists as the Cape Elizabeth Formation. Many of the broken pieces of rock along the shore look like gray petrified logs. Their shape is the function of the geologic forces that formed the Maine coast 400 million years ago. Careful examination of the bedrock reveals subtle variations in color and texture. The rock is compressed sand and mud from the seabed. As these accumulated over time, tidal forces sorted them by size. That sorting can be seen in the rocks. In many places quartz and other hard minerals have been injected into fractures and faults in the bedrock, making for a unique shoreline.

The bluffs above the rocky shore are covered with a thick blanket of rugosa roses and bayberry bushes. In the summer

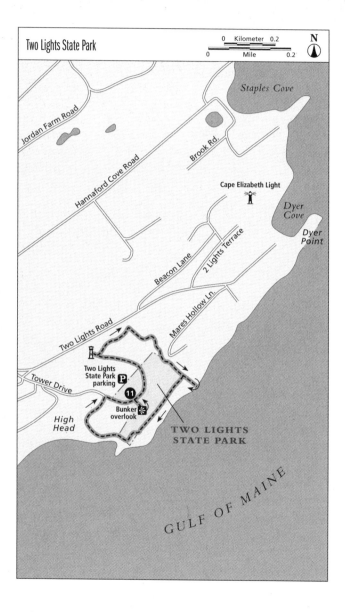

Two Lights State Park

0 Kilometer 0.2
0 Mile 0.2

N

Staples Cove

Jordan Farm Road

Hannaford Cove Road

Brook Rd.

Cape Elizabeth Light

Dyer Cove

Dyer Point

Beacon Lane

2 Lights Terrace

Two Lights Road

Mares Hollow Ln.

Tower Drive

Two Lights State Park parking

P

11

Bunker overlook

TWO LIGHTS STATE PARK

High Head

GULF OF MAINE

they are covered with blooms, while sparrows and warblers flit in and out of view.

Few islands are visible from the hike—Richmond Island to the south. Instead you have an unobstructed view of the open sea. Waves crash into the rock below you as gulls wheel overhead.

Miles and Directions

0.0 Start from the information signs south of the parking area in front of the bunker.

0.2 Walk along the edge of the parking area past the restrooms and the small pond. The trail enters the woods and climbs to the tower.

0.3 Follow the trail northeast from the tower, paralleling Two Lights Road. Turn right at the intersection and descend toward the coast.

0.6 Follow the trail along the eastern boundary of the park, passing several trails. Arrive at the shore.

0.9 Follow the graded trail west along the shore. Beyond High Head, turn inland.

1.0 Arrive at the park road. Turn right to return to the trailhead.

1.1 Just before reaching the trailhead, follow the slate stairs to the top of the bunker with views of the coast.

1.2 Arrive back at the trailhead.

12 Rattlesnake Mountain

Rattlesnake Mountain is a granite ridge north of Sebago Lake amid a jumble of smaller lakes and ponds. The hike climbs along the mountain's southern flank, with views from two open ledges. The trail crosses the oak-covered summit ridge to a series of descending ledges with fine views of the Sebago region. Especially when the trees are leafless, you have views of the White Mountains as well.

Start: Trailhead at back of parking area
Distance: 2.9 miles out and back
Approximate hiking time: 2–3 hours
Difficulty: Moderate
Best season: May–Oct
Trail surface: Woodland path
Land status: Private property, open to the public for hiking

Nearest town: Raymond
Other users: None
Water availability: None
Canine compatibility: Dogs must be under control at all times.
Fees and permits: None
Maps: *DeLorme: Maine Atlas & Gazetteer* map 5; USGS Raymond
Trail contact: None

Finding the trailhead: From exit 63 on the Maine Turnpike (I-95) in Gray, drive west on ME 115 for 6.7 miles. Turn right onto US 302 in North Windham and drive 4.5 miles. Turn right onto ME 85 and drive 7.2 miles. The trailhead parking is at the edge of a field on the left side of the road. The trailhead is at the back of the parking area. GPS: N43 58.432' / W70 28.176'

The Hike

You might think Rattlesnake Mountain was named by a farmer or explorer with an overactive imagination. After all, the nearest rattlesnakes are living in the Blue Hills south of Boston. But, in fact, until the middle of the nineteenth century, there were timber rattlers living in Maine. The broken granite ledges on Rattlesnake Mountain are good habitat for the snakes, so the mountain is probably not named for a mistaken identification.

The Bri-Mar Trail up Rattlesnake Mountain is open to the public due to the generosity of the Huntress family, which owns the land. Please respect the land, and stay on the trail and follow the posted rules.

The hike crosses a field and enters the woods on an old road. After a few tenths of a mile, the trail leaves the woods road and begins to climb steeply through a mostly oak forest. The trail crosses two ledges with views east and south. The ledges are granite. Surprisingly, the Sebago region is mostly underlain by granite. You tend to think of granite and mountains together, but, in fact, several of Maine's largest granite plutons are under lakes or lowlands.

Where the trail levels out to cross the long summit ridge, an unmarked trail leads northwest to a viewpoint. A natural break in the trees offers a fine view of the White Mountains. In the spring and fall, a snowcapped Mount Washington rises above the surrounding peaks, shining like polished marble.

The Bri-Mar Trail crosses the unmarked summit, a bed-size granite dome rising slightly higher than the surrounding forest. Then the trail descends a series of ledges with increasingly open views. The trail ends at a ledge with fine views east, south, and, to a lesser extent, west. Sebago Lake and several ponds lay before you. The hills dividing them make it hard to distinguish Sebago Lake from Jordon Bay from Panther Pond.

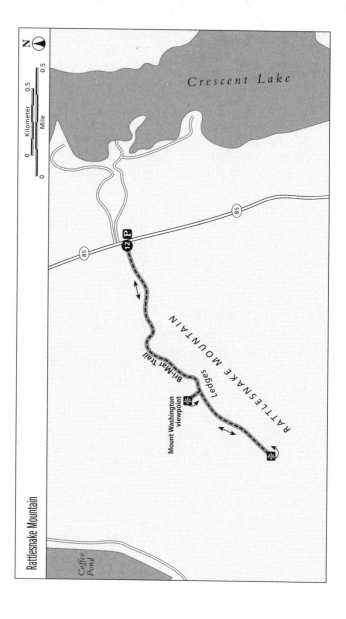

Rattlesnake Mountain

Crescent Lake

Coffee
Pond

RATTLESNAKE MOUNTAIN

Bri-Mar Trail

Ledges

Mount Washington
viewpoint

85

12 P

N

0   Kilometer   0.5

0   Mile   0.5

Across the lake the Saddleback Hills create a serrated line that blends westward into the Oxford Hills and the White Mountains.

Miles and Directions

0.0 Start from the trailhead at the back of the parking area. The trail crosses a field and enters the woods on an old woods road.

0.3 Bear right, leaving the woods road. In 50 feet bear left and begin climbing.

0.4 Turn right, following the trail marked with red arrows. Begin climbing more steeply.

0.7 The trail crosses the first ledge with views east.

0.8 The trail crosses a more open ledge with views east and south.

0.9 An unmarked side trail leads 275 feet northwest to an overlook of Mount Washington.

1.2 Cross the unmarked summit.

1.5 Descend across a series of ledges to an open viewpoint with fine views. To complete the hike, retrace your steps back to the trailhead.

2.9 Arrive back at the trailhead.

13 Wolfe's Neck Woods

This easy hike loops along the shore of Casco Bay past Googins Island and its osprey nest. The shore of the bay is made up of interesting and varied bedrock that changes in character with the changing tide. The shore of the Harraseeket River—actually a long, narrow bay—is a high bluff with several rocky overlooks. The forest in between is oak-pine and hemlock; in each, you will find many mature trees.

Start: White Pines Trailhead on north side of parking area near restrooms

Distance: 2.6-mile loop

Approximate hiking time: 2–4 hours

Difficulty: Easy

Best season: May–Oct

Trail surface: Woodland path

Land status: Wolfe's Neck Woods State Park

Nearest town: Freeport

Other users: None

Water availability: Spigot next to restrooms near trailhead

Canine compatibility: Dogs must be under control at all times.

Fees and permits: State park entrance fee

Maps: *DeLorme: Maine Atlas & Gazetteer* map 6: USGS Freeport

Trail contact: Wolfe's Neck Woods State Park, (207) 865-4465, www.maine.gov/wolfesneckwoods

Finding the trailhead: From exit 22 on I-295, drive east on ME 125 for 0.5 mile into Freeport. Turn right onto US 1 and drive 0.2 mile to Bow Street. There is a very small sign at the intersection directing you toward Wolfe's Neck Woods State Park. Turn left onto Bow Street and drive 1.5 miles to a fork in the road. Bear right at the fork; there is a sign for the park at the fork. Drive 0.9 mile to Wolf Neck Road; there is a sign for the park at the intersection. Turn right onto Wolf Neck Road and drive 2.1 miles to the state park entrance. Turn left into Wolfe's Neck Woods State Park and drive 0.5 mile to the end of the road. The trailhead is on the north side of the parking area next to the restrooms. GPS: N43 49.339' / W70 04.988'

The Hike

For a mile or so, through Freeport, US 1 is a long string of shops, outlets, and restaurants. The sidewalks are crowded with window shoppers and kids eating ice-cream cones. Traffic moves at a crawl, as pedestrians overflow the sidewalks or jaywalk between destinations. Anchoring all this chaos is the L.L. Bean store. Actually, calling it a store doesn't do it justice. It's a campus—several retail buildings with spaces for demonstrations and presentations that takes up an entire block. Some summer days it feels like there are more people in Freeport than in some of Maine's northern counties.

Down a side street, just minutes from the crowds in downtown Freeport, Wolfe's Neck Woods State Park offers quiet hiking along Casco Bay and the Harraseeket River. Wolfe's Neck was named for the family that first settled the area in 1733. The name is variously spelled: Wolfe, Wolf, Woolfe. For example, the state park and the road to the park spell the name differently.

The hike loops around the outside of the park, maximizing the amount of time you spend on the shore. The bedrock along the shore is mostly sedimentary rock that was folded and contorted by tectonic movement. During the folding, granite was injected into the gaps that were created. The result is a shoreline of rock with varied and interesting textures, colors, and feels. The same spot along the shore often looks quite different at high tide than at low tide because different rock is exposed.

Along the Casco Bay Trail, there are several places where steps lead you out onto the rocky shore. One of the first of these is opposite Googins Island. At low tide you can almost walk onto the island, a small lozenge of close-growing evergreens. The island contains one of Wolfe's Neck Woods' osprey nests. You can sit on the shore and watch the ospreys come and go, bringing fish for their nestlings. Between parental stops, you can sit and look out across Casco Bay while the chicks squawk to be fed again. You can't see Portland from the park—a line of islands between Yarmouth and Harpswell bisects the bay—but the view is varied and interesting.

Where the Casco Bay Trail becomes the Harraseeket Trail, the hike turns inland and crosses the wooded neck to the Harraseeket River. Along the way you pass several trails that can be used to make shorter loops. The trail passes through mature forest dominated by large hemlocks. Along the shore the woods are an oak-pine forest with many large white pines. Just the small change in elevation and rockying of the soil changed the forest type.

The trail reaches the river atop a high bluff. The Harraseeket River is actually a long, narrow bay that two small streams empty into at its head. The topography here is like that of the Mid-Coast: long, narrow peninsulas and islands with bays between them, a function of the folding of the sedimentary rock you saw along the Casco Bay Trail. Wolfe's Neck is one of the smaller peninsulas and is situated along the coast, rather than sticking out into the Gulf of Maine.

The trail follows along the Harraseeket River, with several rocky overlooks but no easy water access. Below the bluff you hike along, the shore is a tidal mudflat—not great for exploring anyway. It is, though, a good place to find

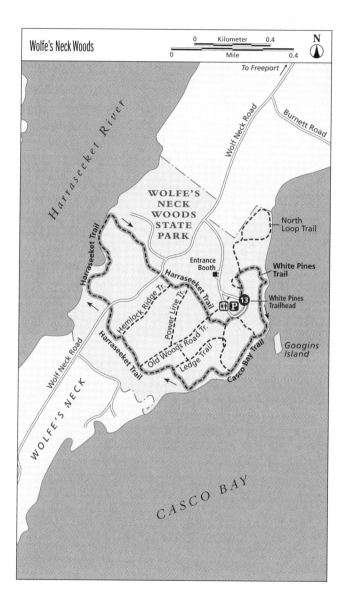

Kilometer

Mile

N

Harraseeket River

To Freeport

Wolf Neck Road

Burnett Road

WOLFE'S
NECK
WOODS
STATE
PARK

North
Loop Trail

Entrance
Booth

Harraseeket Trail

White Pines
Trail

Harraseeket Trail

Hemlock Ridge Tr.

Power Line Tr.

Old Woods Road Tr.

Ledge Trail

White Pines
Trailhead

13

Googins
Island

Casco Bay Trail

Wolf Neck Road

Harraseeket Trail

WOLFE'S NECK

CASCO BAY

shorebirds feeding on the changing tide. The shore along the Harraseeket River is completely different from that along Casco Bay on the other side of Wolfe's Neck. The difference is a result of the folded bedding of the sedimentary bedrock. Along the river the bedding is such that the rock has broken apart, creating high bluffs of loose and crumbly rock.

As you hike back from the river to the parking area, be sure to look for lady slipper orchids and blueberries. They can be found in late spring and midsummer, respectively, throughout the woods here, especially on the high dry sections in the oak-pine forest.

Miles and Directions

0.0 Start from the White Pines Trailhead at the north end of the parking area, next to the restrooms.

0.1 Pass the North Loop Trail.

0.2 The White Pines Trail reaches the shore of Casco Bay.

0.4 The White Pines Trail ends at the Casco Bay Trail. To the right is a short walk back to the parking area; to the left are steps down to the shore. Opposite the shore at this point, across a narrow channel, is Googins Island. On this small island is an osprey nest. Continue straight ahead on the Casco Bay Trail.

0.5 Pass a trail on the right that leads back to the parking area.

0.7 Pass another trail that leads back to the parking area. There is shore access on the left.

0.9 The Casco Bay Trail ends at the Harraseeket Trail. To the left are stairs down to the shore. This is the last shore access on Casco Bay. Turn right onto the Harraseeket Trail.

1.1 Pass the Ledge Trail. This trail can be used to make the shortest loop back to the parking area.

1.2 Pass the Old Woods Road Trail. This trail, too, can be used to make a shorter loop back to the parking area.

1.3 Pass the Hemlock Ridge Trail. This trail can be used to make a shorter loop back to the parking area.

1.6 The Harraseeket Trail reaches a high bluff above the Harraseeket River.

2.0 The trail follows along the shore of the river and then turns away, heading back toward the parking area.

2.6 Follow the Harraseeket Trail back to the parking area, passing several trails along the way. The trail ends at the southeast corner of the parking area.

14 Bradbury Mountain

Bradbury Mountain State Park is crisscrossed with more than 20 miles of trails. Most of the trails are open to hikers, horses, mountain bikers, and cross-country skiers in the winter. The Summit Trail up to the open granite summit is one of the few hiker-only trails. The summit offers fine views east across the flat coastal plain to the ocean. The descent off the mountain follows two of the other hiker-only trails through mature forest that has grown up on former farmland.

Start: Summit Trailhead at north-west corner of parking area, near playground
Distance: 1.2-mile loop
Approximate hiking time: 1–2 hours
Difficulty: Easy
Best season: May–Oct, though park is open year-round
Trail surface: Woodland path
Land status: Bradbury Mountain State Park
Nearest town: Freeport
Other users: Many of the trails are open to mountain biking and skiing in winter.

Water availability: Spigot near trailhead
Canine compatibility: Dogs must be under control at all times.
Fees and permits: State park entrance fee
Maps: *DeLorme: Maine Atlas & Gazetteer* maps 5 and 6; USGS Freeport
Trail contact: Bradbury Mountain State Park, (207) 688-4712, www.bradburymountain.com or www.maine.gov/bradbury mountain

Finding the trailhead: From exit 22 on I-295, drive north on ME 125 for 0.2 mile. Turn left onto Durham Road at the sign for Bradbury Mountain State Park and drive 4.6 miles to ME 9 in Pownal Center. Turn right onto ME 9; there is a sign for the state park at the intersection. Drive 0.5 mile to the park entrance and turn left into Bradbury Mountain State Park. Past the entrance gate, turn right into the parking area. The trailhead is at the northwest corner of the parking area near the playground. GPS: N43 54.014' / W70 10.793'

The Hike

In Britain there is an official definition of a mountain. To be called a mountain, a landform has to be more than 2,000 feet high or stand out from the surrounding country by more than 500 feet. In the United States there used to be a similar definition, but it has fallen out of use. It's almost too bad. If we still had to come up with other designations for less lofty landforms, we could use more descriptive names. Bradbury Mountain, for example, is only 485 feet high—not a mountain by either definition. In Britain it would have to be called something else. "Hill" doesn't quite capture the exposed granite summit that juts east toward the coast. Maybe, it could be "Bradbury Brow." That accurately captures the nature of the landform. It has a rocky summit that offers views in only one direction and slopes gently down on the other, western, side.

Whatever we call it, Bradbury Mountain is a short, steep climb to a fine view. The state park has about 20 miles of trails that snake around and over the mountain. Most trails are open to hikers, horses, mountain bikes, and cross-country skiing in the winter. A few of the trails are hiker-only; this hike traverses three of the four hiker-only trails. Five trails converge on the summit of Bradbury Mountain. On the hike you ascend the Summit Trail—the only one that is hiker-only. The descent is on the Bluff and Terrace Trails, which are also hiker-only.

After this short hike, you may want to explore the South Ridge Trail, the other hiker-only trail, with views to the south. Or you can hike along any of the multiuse trails that wander the woods of the state park. In general, the west-side trails—that include Bradbury Mountain—are better suited for hiking than the east-side trails. Throughout the park, trail junctions are well-marked and the official park map is accurate, so you can wander the trails without having to worry about getting lost.

The area around Bradbury Mountain has not always been the recreational mecca that it is today. As you hike, you pass several old stone walls that crisscross the wooded hillside— a reminder that this land was once cleared for pasture and farming. A further reminder can be found near the end of the hike along the Northern Loop Trail: an old stone cattle pound.

There are also the remains of a small feldspar quarry along the Northern Loop Trail. Feldspar is the most common mineral found in granite. Bradbury Mountain is mostly granite and related pegmatite. The feldspar crystals in pegmatite get fairly large and are therefore quarryable. Small-scale mining operations like the one here were common in southern Maine until the middle of the last century. The feldspar was ground up and used as an abrasive and in ceramics.

Miles and Directions

0.0   Start from the Summit Trailhead at the northwest corner of the parking area, near the playground.

0.2   The hiker-only trail climbs steadily to the open summit, with views south and east. Continue across the summit onto the multiuse Northern Loop Trail.

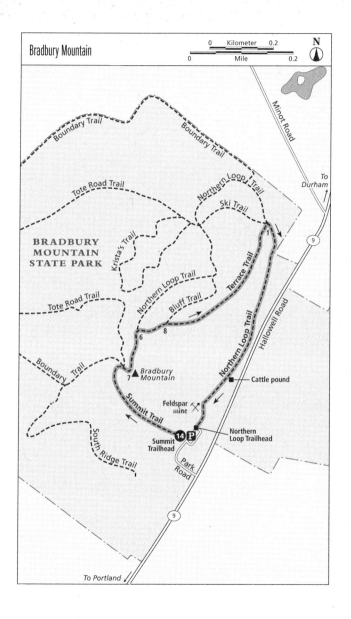

Bradbury Mountain

BRADBURY
MOUNTAIN
STATE PARK

Boundary Trail
Tote Road Trail
Krista's Trail
Northern Loop Trail
Bluff Trail
Tote Road Trail
Boundary Trail
Summit Trail
South Ridge Trail

Northern Loop Trail
Ski Trail
Terrace Trail

Bradbury Mountain
Feldspar mine
Summit Trailhead
Park Road
Cattle pound
Northern Loop Trail
Northern Loop Trailhead
Hallowell Road
Minot Road
To Durham
To Portland

Kilometer
Mile
N

0.3 Arrive at Junction 7. Pass the Tote Road Trail and the Switch-back Trail. Continue to Junction 6. Turn right onto the hiker-only Bluff Trail.

0.4 Arrive at Junction 8. Turn right onto the hiker-only Terrace Trail.

0.7 The Terrace Trail descends gently to end at the multiuse Northern Loop Trail at Junction 1. Turn right onto the Northern Loop Trail.

1.0 The trail passes an old stone cattle pound.

1.1 The trail passes an abandoned feldspar mine.

1.2 Arrive at the east end of the parking area.

15 Long Reach Preserve

The Long Reach Trail loops through boggy lowlands, over rocky ridges, beneath dark evergreens, and along the shore of Long Reach. At the southernmost point of the trail, there is shore access where you can see the towering cliffs across the narrow inlet. A wooded island floats like a battleship halfway across Long Reach. At low tide the island sits in a huge tidal flat; almost no water remains in the reach.

Start: Trailhead on north side of parking area
Distance: 1.8-mile lollipop
Approximate hiking time: 2 hours
Difficulty: Easy
Best season: May–Oct
Trail surface: Woodland path
Land status: Long Reach Preserve
Nearest town: Harpswell

Other users: None
Water availability: None
Canine compatibility: Dogs must be under control at all times.
Fees and permits: None
Maps: *DeLorme: Maine Atlas & Gazetteer* map 6; USGS Orrs Island
Trail contact: Harpswell Heritage Land Trust, (207) 721-1121, http://hhltmaine.org

Finding the trailhead: From exit 31A on I-295, drive south on ME 196 through Topsham 3.2 miles to US 1 north. Merge onto US 1 north and drive 1.8 miles to the Cook's Corner exit, then follow ME 24 south. Drive 7.2 miles and turn right into the parking area for the Trufant-Summerton Ballfield. The trailhead is on the north side of the parking area at a sign for the Long Reach Preserve. GPS: N43 48.932' / W69 55.451'

The Hike

Long Reach is a narrow inlet that nearly bisects Sebascodegan Island. Its northern end is connected by Garnet Strait (crossed by ME 24 2 miles north of Long Reach Preserve) to the New Meadow River. On the west, Long Reach connects to Harpswell Sound by Ewing Narrows. The reach is about 3 miles long and 0.5 mile wide—more narrow at its southern end between Long Reach Mountain and the Long Reach Preserve.

The same folding bedrock that created the region's long, narrow islands, peninsulas, and inlets is evident along the hike. The Long Reach Trail crosses two steep, rocky ridges that run north–south. The bedrock is broken shale injected with dikes of younger granite. The low areas between the ridges support sphagnum bogs. You cross both ridges and skirt between two bogs before reaching the shore of Long Reach.

Depending on the tide, your impression of the reach is likely to be very different. When the tide is in, blue water reflects the 150-foot-high cliffs on Long Reach Mountain. A wooded island floats in the middle of the inlet like a moored battleship, bristling with dark evergreens. On the other hand, when the tide is out, you are confronted with the high cliffs across a huge mudflat. The island sits marooned, with no seawater in sight.

At the southern end of the trail, there is a rocky outcropping of rusty sedimentary rock that gives you access to the shore. From that vantage point, the waters of Long Reach are framed by mature red pines whose branches hang out over the water.

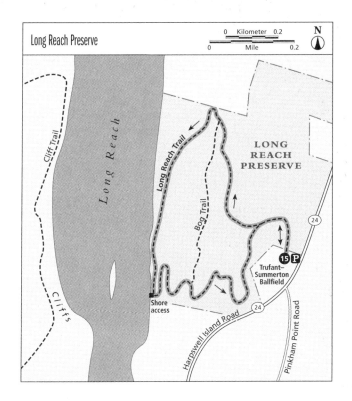

The return hike crosses the first ridge, then drops down to a bog. After skirting between the bog and the nearly vertical ridge, you cross through alders on bog boards. Across the second ridge, the trail winds through old farm fields grown to hardwoods, the fields still delineated by stone walls.

Miles and Directions

0.0 Start from the trailhead on the north side of the parking area.

0.1 Cross a wooden bridge and turn right at the fork. The trail to the left is the return trail.

0.5 The trail climbs a rocky ridge and passes the Bog Trail.

1.0 The trail climbs a second ridge and descends along Long Reach to marked shore access.

1.3 The trail climbs a rocky ridge, then crosses the southern end of a bog on bog boards to the junction with the Bog Trail. Turn right, staying on the Long Reach Trail, to continue the hike.

1.7 Arrive back at the fork. Turn right to return to the trailhead.

1.8 Arrive back at the trailhead.

16 Harpswell Cliffs

The Cliff Trail follows Strawberry Creek—a narrow tidal inlet—to a small waterfall at its head, then passes the salt marsh at the head of Henry Creek before crossing a rocky ridge to the shore of Long Reach. The trail climbs along Long Reach to the top of 150-foot-high cliffs with fine views. Beyond the cliffs the trail descends through woods filled with fairy houses to the trailhead.

Start: Trailhead at north end of parking lot behind Harpswell Town Hall

Distance: 2.2-mile loop

Approximate hiking time: 2 hours

Difficulty: More challenging

Best season: May–Oct

Trail surface: Woodland path

Land status: Town of Harpswell preserve

Nearest town: Harpswell

Other users: None

Water availability: None

Canine compatibility: Dogs must be under control at all times.

Fees and permits: None

Maps: *DeLorme: Maine Atlas & Gazetteer* map 6; USGS Orrs Island

Trail contact: Harpswell Heritage Land Trust, (207) 721-1121, http://hhltmaine.org

Finding the trailhead: From exit 31A on I-295, drive south on ME 196 through Topsham 3.2 miles to US 1 north. Merge onto US 1 north and drive 1.8 miles to the Cook's Corner exit, then follow ME 24 south for 8.5 miles. Turn right onto Mountain Road and drive 1.3 miles. Turn right into the Harpswell Town Hall and park behind the building. The trailhead is at the northwest corner of the parking area. GPS: N43 48.875' / W69 56.580'

The Hike

Behind the Harpswell Town Hall, the Cliff Trail follows Strawberry Creek north to a small waterfall at its head. The creek—really a narrow tidal inlet—winds through a salt marsh hemmed in by dark evergreens.

The trail continues through hardwoods to the salt marsh at the head of Henry Creek. Past the marsh, the trail climbs a rocky ridge of weathered sedimentary rock rusty with age. You then drop down to a bluff along the shore of Long Reach. Turning south, the trail climbs to the top of 150-foot cliffs. There are several open areas with fine views up and down Long Reach. Where the bedrock separated between smooth layers of rock, the cliffs are vertical, dropping away out of sight. The gnarled roots of evergreens cling to the edge of the cliff, the trees hanging out over the precipice.

These cliffs are one of Harpswell's most famous features, but you usually have the trail and the views to yourself. Take a few moments to trace in your mind the convolutions of the surrounding lands and water, watching for ospreys and eagles. This view is as close to a bird's-eye view you can get along Maine's Southern Coast.

Beyond the high cliffs, the trail drops down toward the trailhead. You pass through one of several areas in the preserve that encourage children to build fairy homes. Their efforts add a bit of magic to the forest. Rules for building fairy houses are posted on trees here and at the trailhead.

Miles and Directions

0.0   Start from the trailhead at the northwest corner of the parking lot behind the Harpswell Town Hall.

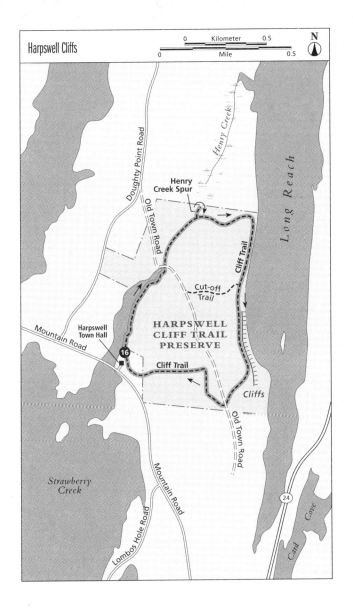

Kilometer

0   0.5

Mile

0   0.5

N

Henry Creek

Long Reach

Doughty Point Road

Old Town Road

Henry Creek Spur

Cliff Trail

Cut-off Trail

HARPSWELL CLIFF TRAIL PRESERVE

Mountain Road

Harpswell Town Hall

16

Cliff Trail

Cliffs

Old Town Road

Strawberry Creek

Mountain Road

24

Card Cove

Lombos Hole Road

0.3 The Cliff Trail follows Strawberry Creek to its head, where there is a small waterfall. Cross Old Town Road and continue on the Cliff Trail.

0.6 A side trail leads 150 feet to Henry Creek Marsh.

0.9 The Cliff Trail climbs over a ridge and descends toward Long Reach.

1.2 Pass a trail on the right.

1.4 Reach the highest cliffs.

1.6 The trail follows atop the cliffs, then turns west and descends.

2.1 The Cliff Trail ends at the recycling center.

2.2 Cross the lawn in front of the recycling center and follow the blazes around the town hall to arrive back at the trailhead.

17 Giant's Stairs

The Giant's Stairs are a break in the rocky coast of Bailey Island where a natural staircase of basalt leads from the trail down into the crashing surf. This easy walk passes other formations such as Pinnacle Rock. A short clamber over the rocks from the end of the graded trail leads to The Gully, a narrow inlet off Little Harbor.

Start: Giant's Stairs parking area next to church at corner of Washington Avenue and Ocean Street
Distance: 0.8 mile out and back
Approximate hiking time: 1 hour
Difficulty: Easy
Best season: May–Oct
Trail surface: Graded trail and rocky shoreline
Land status: Giant's Stairs Preserve
Nearest town: Harpswell

Other users: None
Water availability: None
Canine compatibility: Dogs must be under control at all times.
Fees and permits: None
Maps: *DeLorme: Maine Atlas & Gazetteer* map 6; USGS Bailey Island
Trail contact: Harpswell Heritage Land Trust, (207) 721-1121, http://hhltmaine.org

Finding the trailhead: From exit 31A on I-295, drive south on ME 196 through Topsham 3.2 miles to US 1 north. Merge onto US 1 north and drive 1.8 miles to the Cook's Corner exit, then follow ME 24 south. Drive 14.7 miles, crossing Sebascodegan and Orr's Islands, and onto Bailey Island near the end of ME 24. Continue straight onto Hugh Avenue and drive 0.3 mile. Turn left onto Washington Avenue and drive 0.1 mile to the marked parking area on the left at Ocean Street where Washington Avenue makes a sharp right. The hike begins with a walk down Ocean Street to the shore. GPS: N43 43.581' / W69 59.661'. On Sundays and when the parking area is full, you will need to park 0.3 mile farther along Washington Avenue at the McIntosh Lot parking area.

The Hike

The drive to the Giant's Stairs down ME 24 crosses an increasingly narrow chain of islands. Orr's and Bailey Islands are less than a mile wide. The bridge that connects the two islands is a unique cribwork bridge. Long granite blocks were laid on a natural reef in an open cribwork pattern to allow the strong and substantial tides to flow through the bridge. The rush of the tide through Will's Gut would have destroyed a conventional bridge. The cribwork bridge has lasted since 1928—with substantial repairs to widen and shore it up completed in 2010.

Along much of Maine's Mid-Coast, the bedrock is sedimentary with dikes of igneous rock injected into it. Mostly the dikes are granite, but not always. The Giant's Stairs is a basalt dike that runs perpendicular to the grain of the older sedimentary bedrock. Over time the basalt weathered more than the bedrock into what looks like a black staircase from the trail down into the crashing surf.

The Giant's Stairs are about halfway along the graded gravel path that follows the rocky shore. To your right, wild bushes hide the houses along Hugh Avenue; to your left, the sea batters the rocky bluff you hike atop. The shoreline is an irregular line of sedimentary rock broken into uneven blocks and fins of thinly layered shale that when wet looks like frozen mud.

A plaque marks the top of the Giant's Stairs. The tarnished metal bolted to a boulder dates back to 1910. From here there are fine views of the rocks and small islands in the bay between Bailey Island and Phippsburg.

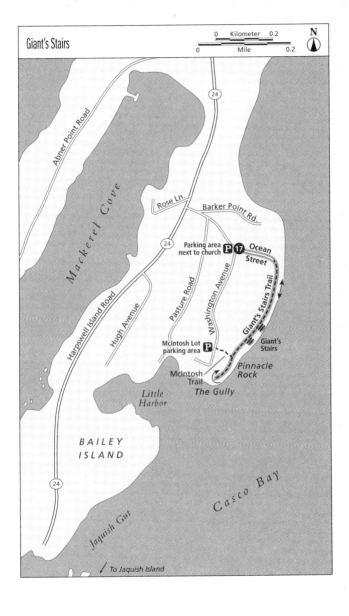

Giant's Stairs

0 Kilometer 0.2
0 Mile 0.2

N

Abner Point Road

Mackerel Cove

Rose Ln.
Barker Point Rd.

24

Parking area next to church
P 17
Ocean Street

Harpswell Island Road

Hugh Avenue

Pasture Road

Washington Avenue

Giant's Stairs Trail

McIntosh Lot parking area
P

Giant's Stairs

McIntosh Trail

Pinnacle Rock

The Gully

Little Harbor

BAILEY ISLAND

Casco Bay

24

Jaquish Gut

To Jaquish Island

The trail continues along the shore past Pinnacle Rock, a fin of bedrock that juts from rocks near the water. On your right a short trail leads through low beach shrubs to Hugh Avenue.

From this point you can follow blazes on the rock around a headland to The Gully. During storms, surf rushing into the narrow defile is forced upward to spray on the cliffs. When the sea is calmer, the tide eases in and out of The Gully as sea ducks bob on the swells in Little Harbor. Dark spruce-covered islands with naked rock shores and bedrock reefs congregate in Jaquish Gut. There is so much to see on this hike that it may seem much longer than it actually is.

Miles and Directions

0.0 Start from the parking area next to the church at the corner of Washington Avenue and Ocean Street. Walk down Ocean Street.

0.1 At the end of Ocean Street, a marked trail leads south along the shore.

0.2 On the left is a plaque on a block of stone at the top of the Giant's Stairs.

0.3 Pass the McIntosh Trail that leads 250 feet to Washington Avenue. On the left is Pinnacle Rock. Continue straight ahead.

0.4 The trail ends at the rocky shore. Follow the red blazes around a small point to The Gully. To complete the hike, return the way you came.

0.8 Arrive back at the trailhead.

18 Hamilton Audubon Sanctuary

A series of looping trails follow the spruce-covered shore of Back Cove and the narrow rocky channel between Foster Point and Williams Island. The hike also passes two small ponds and meadows. There are several places along the trails where you can access the shore. Although at low tide much of Back Cove is a mudflat, it is still quite scenic.

Start: Trailhead across Foster Point Road from parking area

Distance: 2.7-mile multi-loop

Approximate hiking time: 2–3 hours

Difficulty: Easy

Best season: May–Oct

Trail surface: Woodland path

Land status: Hamilton Audubon Sanctuary

Nearest town: Bath

Other users: None

Water availability: None

Canine compatibility: No dogs allowed

Fees and permits: None

Maps: *DeLorme: Maine Atlas & Gazetteer* map 6; USGS Orrs Island

Trail contact: Maine Audubon, (207) 781-2330, http://maineaudubon.org/find-us/hamilton-sanctuary

Finding the trailhead: From exit 31A on I-295, drive through Topsham on ME 196 3.2 miles. Merge onto US 1 north and drive 5 miles. Exit onto New Meadows Road, turn right, and drive 0.6 mile. Go straight across State Street onto Foster Point Road and drive 3.4 miles. The preserve parking is on the right at the sign. The trailhead is across the road from the parking area. GPS: N43 51.996' / W69 53.276'

The Hike

The hike first follows the Red Trail across a meadow that slopes down to Back Cove. Meadows like this one are a great place to find butterflies and summer birds. They also harbor ticks. When you walk through the screen of trees to the shore, make sure to check yourself for unwanted hitchhikers.

From the Red Trail, follow the Blue Trail down across the bridge over a narrow inlet that looks more like a creek. Follow the Blue Trail as it loops up to and around several small points. Dappled sunlight filters through the evergreens that grow widely spaced enough that you always have a view of the cove. At the junction with the Yellow Trail, a small pond is slowly turning into a marshy meadow. At some point in the past, this pond was probably in a pasture.

The Green Trail passes a second small pond within sight of Back Cove and then reenters the woods. As you hike along the outside of a point, you pass marshy ground and many snags leaning this way and that. Where the trail turns south, the shore becomes a low rock face. Across a narrow channel is Williams Island. The forest along this section is close-growing spruce, limiting views. The forest here is very different from that at the beginning of the hike, darker and less inviting.

As you wind your way back to the trailhead, you pass back through the several types of forest, each with its own scent. The dark smell of dry spruce gives way to the green smell of pine and moss. Sometimes it isn't an expansive view or the wildlife that you remember later, but the particular scent of a mossy glen or tidal mudflat baking in the sun.

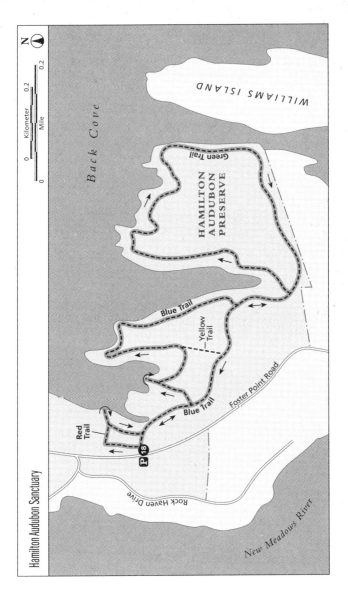

Hamilton Audubon Sanctuary

Miles and Directions

0.0   Start from the trailhead across Foster Point Road from the parking area. Follow the Red Trail through the meadow toward Back Cove.

0.1   Arrive at Back Cove. Continue south on the Red Trail.

0.2   Turn left onto the Blue Trail.

0.3   Turn left at the fork in the Blue Trail. The right-hand fork will be your return trail.

0.5   The Blue Trail loops out a small point in Back Cove. At the pond, pass the Yellow Trail, staying left on the Blue Trail.

1.1   The Blue Trail loops out a larger point, then heads south along an inlet. Turn left onto the Green Trail.

1.2   Turn left at the fork in the Green Trail.

1.8   The Green Trail follows along a narrow inlet between Foster Point and Williams Island.

2.2   Arrive back at the fork in the Green Trail. Go straight to return to the trailhead.

2.3   Arrive back at the Blue Trail. Bear left to return to the trailhead.

2.4   Pass the Yellow Trail.

2.5   Arrive back at the fork in the Blue Trail. Bear left to return to the trailhead.

2.7   Arrive back at the trailhead.

19 Thorne Head

Thorne Head Preserve offers miles of hiking trails that crisscross old farmland and pastures, follow the shore of the Kennebec River as it slides silently through The Narrows, and climbs to a rocky overlook of the wide, island-filled confluence of the Kennebec River and Whiskeag Creek. The hike described here follows most, but not all, of the trails in the preserve.

Start: Overlook Trailhead at north end of parking area, next to information kiosk
Distance: 2.5-mile multi-loop
Approximate hiking time: 2 hours
Difficulty: Moderate due to steep sections of Stone Steps and Mushroom Cap Trails
Best season: May–Oct, but trail system is used year-round
Trail surface: Woodland path

Land status: Thorne Head Preserve
Nearest town: Bath
Other users: None
Water availability: None
Canine compatibility: Dogs must be on a leash at all times.
Fees and permits: None
Maps: *DeLorme: Maine Atlas & Gazetteer* map 6; USGS Bath
Trail contact: Kennebec Estuary Land Trust, (207) 442-8400, www.kennebecestuary.org

Finding the trailhead: From exit 31A on I-295, drive south on ME 196 through Topsham 3.2 miles to US 1 north. Merge onto US 1 north and drive 7.1 miles into Bath and exit US 1 onto High Street. Turn left onto High Street and drive 2.5 miles to the gravel end of the road. High Street ends at the parking area for Thorne Head. The trailhead is at the north end of the parking area. GPS: N43 56.593' / W69 49.110'

The Hike

Shipbuilding has always been important to the lower Kennebec River. The first settlers to the region—and England's first attempt create a permanent settlement in what is now the United States—founded Popham near the mouth of the Kennebec. They built the first ship constructed in Britain's North American colonies.

Later, a thriving shipbuilding industry grew along the straight, deep section of river at Bath. The site was ideal, with its deep port and proximity to the various woods needed to construct the era's ships. Even though ships are now steel, the industry remains.

Thorne Head itself was logged several times over the centuries for oak and especially white pine. Much of the preserve was pasture until the early twentieth century. Along the hike you can find stone walls that once separated one pasture from another. As you hike beneath the towering pines and oaks, it's hard to imagine this rocky landscape as anything other than forest.

From the north end of the Overlook Trail, you have a fine view of the island-filled confluence of the Kennebec River and Whiskeag Creek. Beneath the overlook the river jogs east and rushes through The Narrows. From there, for the next 4 miles, the Kennebec runs straight and deep between Bath and Woolwich. Watch for eagles and ospreys fishing in the river or perched atop the tall pines along the shore.

The hike makes several loops around the preserve, visiting all of the habitats found here and following the river and creek. Feel free to deviate from the described hike to lengthen or shorten it—or just to revisit your favorite section.

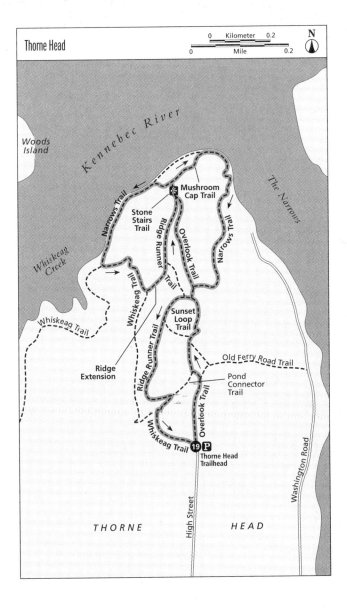

Thorne Head

Kennebec River

Woods Island

Whiskeag Creek

The Narrows

Narrows Trail

Stone Stairs Trail

Ridge Runner Trail

Mushroom Cap Trail

Overlook Trail

Narrows Trail

Whiskeag Trail

Sunset Loop Trail

Ridge Runner Trail

Ridge Extension

Whiskeag Trail

Old Ferry Road Trail

Pond Connector Trail

Overlook Trail

Whiskeag Trail

19 P Thorne Head Trailhead

High Street

Washington Road

THORNE   HEAD

Kilometer 0.2

Mile 0.2

N

Miles and Directions

0.0 Start from the Overlook Trailhead at the north end of the parking area next to the information kiosk.

0.2 Pass a marshy pond on your left. Just beyond the pond, pass the Pond Connector Trail.

0.3 Pass the southern end of the Sunset Loop Trail.

0.4 Pass the northern end of the Sunset Loop Trail on the left and then the Narrows Trail on the right.

0.6 The Overlook Trail ends at an overlook of the Kennebec River. Follow the Stone Stairs Trail northwest off the overlook.

0.7 Turn left, continuing to descend the Stone Stairs Trail.

0.8 The Stone Stairs Trail ends at the Narrows Trail along the bank of the Kennebec River. Turn left.

1.1 The Narrows Trail follows the shore of Whiskeag Creek, then turns inland and ends at the Whiskeag Trail. Turn left.

1.2 Turn left onto the Ridge Runner Trail.

1.4 Arrive back at the overlook. Continue across the overlook and down the Stone Stairs Trail again.

1.5 Turn right onto the Mushroom Cap Trail.

1.6 Turn right onto the Narrows Trail.

1.9 The Narrows Trail follows the shore of the Kennebec River, where it passes through The Narrows, then climbs away from the river.

2.0 Turn left onto the Overlook Trail, then right onto the Sunset Loop Trail.

2.1 Turn left onto the Ridge Runner Trail. In 200 feet, pass the southern end of the Sunset Loop Trail.

2.3 Arrive at the shore of the pond. Turn left, staying on the Ridge Runner Trail.

2.4 Turn left onto the Whiskeag Trail.

2.5 Arrive back at the trailhead.

20 Sprague Pond Loop

The Sprague Pond Loop follows Burnt Ledge south between swampy lowlands. The trail crosses a small stream that flows out of a bog and cascades down rounded bedrock, then drops down from the falls to Sprague Pond, a spring-fed pond surrounded by thick woods. The return hike crosses and follows several ledges, including one with a view of the surrounding country and another covered with blueberries.

Start: Sprague Pond Trailhead on south side of Basin Road just west of American chestnut tree farm

Distance: 5.5-mile lollipop

Approximate hiking time: 3-4 hours

Difficulty: More challenging

Best season: May-Oct

Trail surface: Woodland path

Land status: Basin Preserve

Nearest town: Phippsburg

Other users: None

Water availability: None

Canine compatibility: No dogs allowed

Fees and permits: None

Maps: *DeLorme: Maine Atlas & Gazetteer* map 6; USGS Phippsburg

Trail contact: Basin Preserve of the Nature Conservancy, www .nature.org/ourinitiatives/ regions/northamerica/ unitedstates/maine

Finding the trailhead: From exit 31A on I-295, drive south on ME 196 through Topsham 3.2 miles to US 1 north. Merge onto US 1 north and drive 7.1 miles into Bath and exit US 1 onto ME 209. Turn right and drive 7.3 miles into Phippsburg. Turn right onto Basin Road and drive 0.7 mile. The trailhead parking is on the left at the sign just past the American chestnut tree farm. The trailhead is at the east end of the parking area. GPS: N43 48.441' / W69 49.879'

The Hike

The Sprague Pond Loop is not the shortest hike to Sprague Pond, but sometimes it is the journey that is important, not the destination. The trail follows Burnt Ledge south between low, boggy areas. Much of the hike is on these granite ledges. A lot of the granite in Phippsburg is a type known as pegmatite. Pegmatite forms late in the crystallization process of the formation of a granite pluton—made out of leftovers including minerals and rare elements that don't readily crystallize into regular granite. Pegmatites often are a good source of semiprecious gems like aquamarine, beryl, and tourmaline. There are many abandoned quarries in Phippsburg; look for them along the hike.

The plant life on the ledges is more like that found Downeast than in southern Maine: gnarled evergreens, lichens, and blueberries. The thin soils on the ledges lead to very different forests than those found in the lowlands between the ridges.

The trail crosses a small stream between the natural bedrock dam that forced the water to spread out into a good-size bog and a series of small waterfalls. Beneath mature pines the stream flows over a series of descending domes of rock. The stream flows straight down to Sprague Pond, but the trail loops south before dropping down to the pond.

Sprague Pond is a spring-fed teardrop surrounded by a mixed forest. The trail follows along its west shore between the pond and a high bluff. Beyond Sprague Pond the trail climbs the bluff and follows a tiny stream that flows out of a series of boulders and bluffs.

The trail leads up out of the mossy woods and onto a dry ledge. An unmarked side trail climbs to an outcrop with

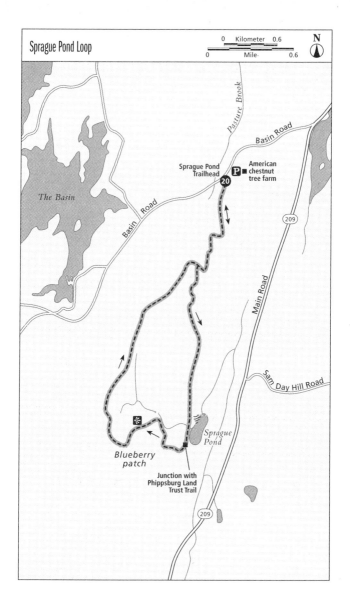

Sprague Pond Loop

0   Kilometer   0.6

0   Mile·   0.6

N

Pasture Brook

Basin Road

Sprague Pond
Trailhead

American
chestnut
tree farm

P

20

209

The Basin

Basin Road

Main Road

Sam Day Hill Road

Sprague
Pond

Blueberry
patch

Junction with
Phippsburg Land
Trust Trail

209

209

a 360-degree view of the surrounding country. Past that the trail crosses a blueberry-covered ledge. The trail turns north and one after another follows semi-open ledges toward the trailhead.

Miles and Directions

0.0 Start from the trailhead next to the sign at the east end of the parking area.

0.8 Turn left at the fork in the trail. The right-hand trail will be your return trail.

2.0 The trail passes a waterfall, where a stream drains out of a bog.

2.2 Reach Sprague Pond.

2.4 At the south end of Sprague Pond, pass the Phippsburg Land Trust Trail that leads to a trailhead on ME 209. Bear right and climb away from the pond.

2.9 On the right is a rocky outcrop that you can climb for a fine view of the surrounding country.

3.1 The trail passes through an especially rich blueberry patch.

4.7 Arrive back at the fork. Turn left to return to the trailhead.

5.5 Arrive back at the trailhead.

21 Cox's Head

This short hike leads to the rocky summit of Cox's Head, with fine views of the mouth of the Kennebec River and Port Popham. Along the hike you pass huge old trees, climb a rocky ridge, and pass a small spring-fed pond.

Start: Trailhead on north side of Green Point Road
Distance: 0.6 mile out and back with a loop
Approximate hiking time: 1 hour
Difficulty: More challenging
Best season: May–Oct
Trail surface: Woodland path
Land status: Wilber Preserve
Nearest town: Phippsburg
Other users: None

Water availability: None
Canine compatibility: Dogs must be under control at all times.
Fees and permits: None
Maps: DeLorme: Maine Atlas & Gazetteer map 6; USGS Phippsburg
Trail contact: Phippsburg Land Trust, (207) 443-5993, www .phippsburglandtrust.org

Finding the trailhead: From exit 31A on I-295, drive south on ME 196 through Topsham 3.2 miles to US 1 north. Merge onto US 1 north and drive 7.1 miles into Bath and exit US 1 onto ME 209. Turn right and drive 13.2 miles. Turn left onto Parker Head Road and drive 0.9 mile. Turn right onto Cox's Head Road and drive 0.8 mile. Cox's Head Road becomes the gravel Green Point Road at the preserve sign. Drive 0.2 mile. The trailhead parking is on the left (and at the end of the road). The trailhead is at the back of the parking area. GPS: N43 45.944' / W69 47.306'

The Hike

Cox Head juts out into the Kennebec River near its mouth. The river's channel is narrowed considerably between Cox Head and Long Island. As a result, the river is nearly 100 feet deep. From the overlook atop Cox Head, you can watch the dark Kennebec rush past toward the Gulf of Maine.

Across Atkins Bay is Popham Beach and the fort of the same name. The Civil War–era fort was built of granite blocks mined off nearby islands, but it was never completed. American use of Popham Beach dates all the way back to 1607. Popham Colony was chartered the same year as Jamestown (in Virginia) and a dozen years before the *Mayflower* landed at Plymouth. The colony only survived two years before it was abandoned. In fact, the exact location of the settlement was unknown until 1994. Today the tiny peninsula contains the remains of Fort Popham, the more modern Fort Baldwin, a small summer community, and Popham Beach State Park. The view from Cox Head of this historic area is among the best in the state. The Kennebec River rushes between headlands to the sea, and a curve of sandy beach disappears behind the peninsula. Out in the Gulf of Maine, blocky islands dot the blue water. In the foreground the tidal mudflats of Atkins Bay attract noisy gulls and clam diggers.

The hike to this great view is less than half a mile. You climb through a stand of ancient gnarled apple trees and past an open woodland to a rocky climb. The trail passes a small spring-fed pond that was used as a local water source for many generations—all the way back to at least the Revolutionary War—and then you are on the bedrock summit.

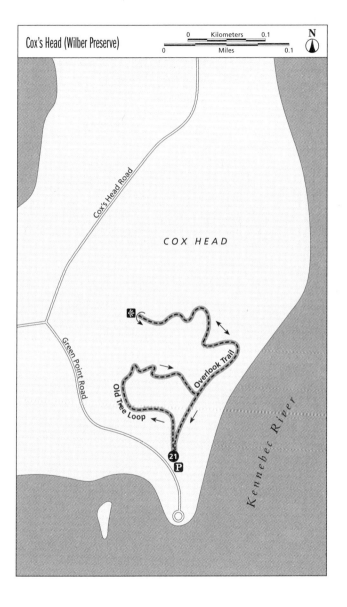

Miles and Directions

0.0 Start from the trailhead at the back of the parking area. In 70 feet, turn left onto the Old Tree Loop.

0.2 Turn left onto the Overlook Trail.

0.4 Arrive at the overlook. To complete the hike, follow the Overlook Trail back to the trailhead.

0.6 Arrive back at the trailhead.

22 Spirit Pond

Spirit Pond is separated from the sea on the east by a narrow isthmus. To the south a low hill is the only thing between it and the tidal marshes at the mouth of the Morse River. The hike follows along the west shore of the pond to the Morse River. You then head north, following the high ground next to the wide salt marsh that the Morse River flows through. The land is part of Popham Beach State Park, but it feels a world away from the crowds on the beaches.

Start: Trailhead on east side of parking area
Distance: 2.5-mile loop
Approximate hiking time: 2 hours
Difficulty: Easy
Best season: May–Oct
Trail surface: Woodland path
Land status: State-owned land managed as Spirit Pond Preserve by Phippsburg Land Trust
Nearest town: Phippsburg

Other users: None
Water availability: None
Canine compatibility: Dogs must be under control at all times.
Fees and permits: None
Maps: *DeLorme: Maine Atlas & Gazetteer* map 6; USGS Phippsburg
Trail contact: Phippsburg Land Trust, (207) 443-5993, www .phippsburglandtrust.org

Finding the trailhead: From exit 31A on I-295, drive south on ME 196 through Topsham 3.2 miles to US 1 north. Merge onto US 1 north and drive 7.1 miles into Bath and exit US 1 onto ME 209. Turn right and drive 11.3 miles to the junction with ME 216. Turn left, staying on ME 209, and drive 1.5 miles. The trailhead parking is on the right. The trailhead is on the east side of the parking area. GPS: N43 45.212' / W69 48.754'

The Hike

Spirit Pond sits only a few feet above sea level, but it's enough to keep the water fresh. To the east of the pond, across a narrow isthmus, is Atkins Bay. South of Spirit Pond is the tidal marsh at the mouth of the Morse River. The river, one branch of which flows out of Spirit Pond, is tidal all the way up to the dam at the pond's head.

Spirit Pond is named for the three rune stones found near the pond in 1971. The stones contain a map and fifteen lines of runic text, and allegedly tell the story of Vikings trying to save their ship in a storm. They are widely believed to be a fraud or hoax, but there are so few examples of such runes that it is impossible to know for sure. If the stones were authentic, it would be an interesting coincidence that they were found less than a mile from the site of the first attempt by the English to establish a permanent settlement in what is now the United States.

The hike first reaches Spirit Pond at the site of an old cemetery. A handful of rough markers made of native stone lean this way and that beneath the trees on the shore of the pond. As you follow along the shore of Spirit Pond, there are several more places where you can reach the water.

The last is at the site of an old mill dam at the head of the pond. Water streams through a breach in the dam down broken bedrock to the Morse River. The hike follows the river to where the east branch drains out of an extensive salt marsh. A side trail gives you the option of more views of the marsh.

On the hike back to the trailhead, even if the main trail seems dry, take the bypass. The hike on this trail is more interesting than hiking out the abandoned road.

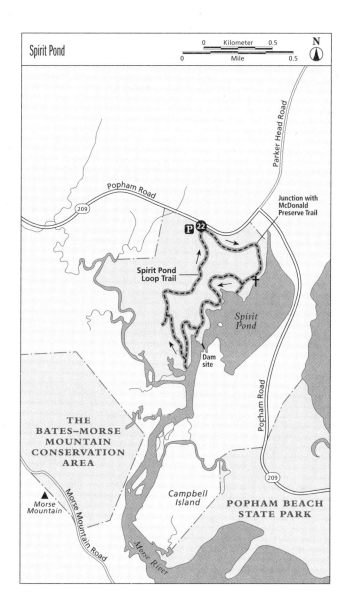

Spirit Pond

0 — Kilometer — 0.5
0 — Mile — 0.5

N

Parker Head Road

Popham Road

209

Junction with
McDonald
Preserve Trail

P 22

Spirit Pond
Loop Trail

✝

Spirit
Pond

Dam
site

THE
BATES–MORSE
MOUNTAIN
CONSERVATION
AREA

Morse
Mountain

Morse Mountain Road

Campbell
Island

POPHAM BEACH
STATE PARK

Popham Road

209

Morse River

Miles and Directions

0.0 Start from the trailhead on the east side of the parking area.

0.3 Arrive at a T-intersection. The left-hand trail leads around the north end of Spirit Pond in the McDonald Preserve. Turn right, staying on the Spirit Pond Loop Trail.

0.4 A short side trail leads to a small cemetery on the shore of Spirit Pond.

0.6 A side trail leads 250 feet to the shore of Spirit Pond.

0.9 Turn left at the junction.

1.2 A side trail leads 350 feet to the site of the dam where the Morse River flows out of Spirit Pond.

1.6 A short side trail leads to an overlook of the Morse River marshes.

1.9 Another short side trail leads to an overlook of the Morse River marshes. Turn right to head back to the trailhead.

2.0 The trail follows a muddy road bypass. Even if the trail ahead doesn't look muddy, take the bypass. It is the more interesting route.

2.5 Arrive back at the trailhead.

23 Seawall Beach

The hike follows a private road up and over Morse Mountain to Seawall Beach. The beach is a wide crescent of fine sand between the Morse and Sprague Rivers, with several nearby rocky islands. Because there is no way to drive to the beach, it is never crowded. The view from ledges near Morse Mountain's summit are expansive, taking in miles of coastline.

Start: Gate beyond parking lot on Morse Mountain Road
Distance: 4.1 miles out and back
Approximate hiking time: 2–3 hours, plus time spent exploring the beach
Difficulty: More challenging
Best season: May–Oct
Trail surface: Private road and sand beach
Land status: Bates–Morse Mountain Conservation Area
Nearest town: Phippsburg

Other users: None
Water availability: None
Canine compatibility: No dogs allowed
Fees and permits: None
Maps: *DeLorme: Maine Atlas & Gazetteer* map 6; USGS Phippsburg
Trail contact: Bates–Morse Mountain Conservation Area. In season there are volunteers at the trailhead, but there is no contact phone number or web address.

Finding the trailhead: From exit 31A on I-295, drive south on ME 196 through Topsham 3.2 miles to US 1 north. Merge onto US 1 north and drive 7.1 miles into Bath and exit US 1 onto ME 209. Turn right and drive 11.3 miles to the junction with ME 216. Drive straight, onto ME 216, and continue 0.8 mile. Turn left onto Morse Mountain Road and drive 0.1 mile. Trailhead parking is in the lot on the left before the gate across the road. The hike begins at the gate. GPS: N43 44.688' / W69 50.242'

The Hike

The hike to Seawall Beach follows a private road to and over Morse Mountain. The road drops down to and crosses a salt marsh, with the Sprague River flowing through it. In the distance you can almost see the beach beyond the widening marsh.

Across the marsh the trail begins to climb through mature evergreens. The thick canopy and needle-covered ground make the woods cool and fragrant. As you climb, the trees thin. The forest understory is more varied and dense.

Summit Circle leads up to the summit of Morse Mountain, where a short trail leads out onto ledges with an expansive view. Spread out beneath you is almost the entire serpentine length of the Sprague River. On the other side of the river's course is Small Point. All along the coast is a wide arc of pale sand.

The road winds across the top of Morse Mountain through mostly spruce and then descends toward Seawall Beach. The trail levels out and passes next to the Sprague River's salt marsh before winding through the woods to the beach.

Seawall Beach is a wide expanse of fine pale sand between the Sprague and Morse Rivers. Across the mouth of both rivers, the beach continues. This is the largest beach system along Maine's Mid-Coast. The size and location of the beaches are a result of the Kennebec River and tidal forces delivering and sorting an ice age worth of glacial debris.

Behind the beach, rocky bluffs separate the woods from the beach and screen the few building along the coast here. Take time to explore the beach from one river mouth to the other. There are several photogenic nearshore islands and

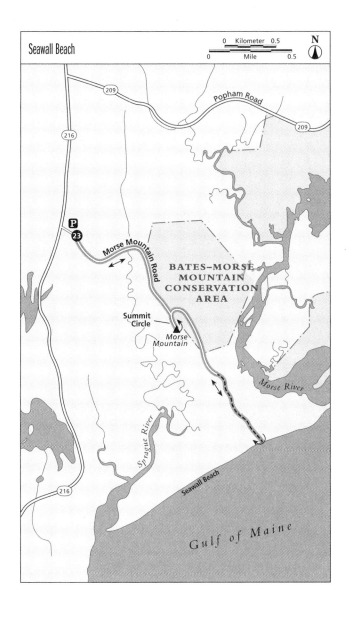

Seawall Beach

0 Kilometer 0.5
0 Mile 0.5

N

209

Popham Road

209

216

P
23

Morse Mountain Road

BATES–MORSE
MOUNTAIN
CONSERVATION
AREA

Summit
Circle

Morse
Mountain

Morse River

Sprague River

216

Seawall Beach

Gulf of Maine

extensive salt marshes near the rivers. Don't forget to study the sand: The beaches along this section of coast are mostly ground granite with lots of garnet and other colorful minerals mixed in.

Miles and Directions

0.0 Start from the gate across Morse Mountain Road.

0.2 Morse Mountain Road crosses a hill then descends to a causeway over the Sprague River.

0.9 Across the Sprague River, the road climbs through mature forest to Summit Circle. Turn right onto Summit Circle.

1.0 Hike up the road and follow the sign out a short trail to open ledges with fine views of the coast and the Sprague River. To continue the hike, return the way you came to Morse Mountain Road.

1.1 Turn right back onto Morse Mountain Road.

2.1 The road descends—steeply at times—to the beach. At the end of the road, a short trail leads out through the sand to the beach. To complete the hike, follow Morse Mountain Road back the way you came.

4.1 Arrive back at the trailhead.

24 Higgins Mountain

Higgins Mountain is only 259 feet high, but offers fine views of the surrounding country, including Robinhood Cove and much of Georgetown Island. The trail crosses the semi-open summit through pitch pines, lichen, and blueberries.

Start: Trailhead on west side of ME 127

Distance: 0.6-mile loop

Approximate hiking time: 1 hour

Difficulty: More challenging

Best season: May–Oct

Trail surface: Woodland path and granite bedrock

Land status: Higgins Mountain Preserve

Nearest Town: Georgetown

Other users: Hunting allowed in season

Water availability: None

Canine compatibility: Yes

Fees and permits: None

Maps: *DeLorme: Maine Atlas & Gazetteer* map 6; USGS Phippsburg

Trail contact: Kennebec Estuary Land Trust, (207) 442-8400, www.kennebecestuary.org

Finding the trailhead: From exit 31A on I-295, take ME 196 through Topsham 3.2 miles. Merge onto US 1 north and drive 8.1 miles to Woolwich. Exit onto ME 127 south and drive 8 miles. Just before reaching Georgetown village, Higgins Mountain Preserve is on the right. There is parking on the wide shoulder in front of the preserve sign. The trailhead is the north trail. GPS: N43 48.901' / W69 45.406'

The Hike

Higgins Mountain at 259 feet isn't really high enough to warrant being called a mountain. But it is one of the highest points on Georgetown Island, and its summit looks and feels like the much higher mountains on Mount Desert Island.

The trail slabs along the east face of the mountain, then climbs over broken granite toward the summit. The mountain is a granite mass that was intruded into the older metamorphic rock of the surrounding country around 400 million years ago. The trail crosses the semi-open dome of the summit through pitch pines. The summit is so open because of the thin, acidic soil and also a fire in 2003. Blueberries grow between the lichen-covered slabs of bedrock where soil collects.

The trail doesn't cross the actual summit—it's to the west of the trail, where the mountain is more heavily wooded. Near the south end of the summit dome, there is an overlook with fine views. You can see Robinhood Cove, much of Georgetown Island, and the sea beyond. Robinhood Cove isn't named for the famous English do-gooder. Rather, it's named for Robert Hood, the sachem of the local Abenaki Indians from whom early settlers acquired Georgetown Island.

The view from Higgins Mountain is almost entirely forested. Until a few generations ago, the scene would have been very different. Much of Georgetown was open farmland or pasture, but as in much of Maine, changes in the farming economy made it less economical to work the land.

As you sit on a boulder eating blueberries, you can think about the vast sweep of history before you. Or you can just enjoy the salt on the breeze and the sweet fruit. Either way, it is a charming little hike over a beautiful mountain.

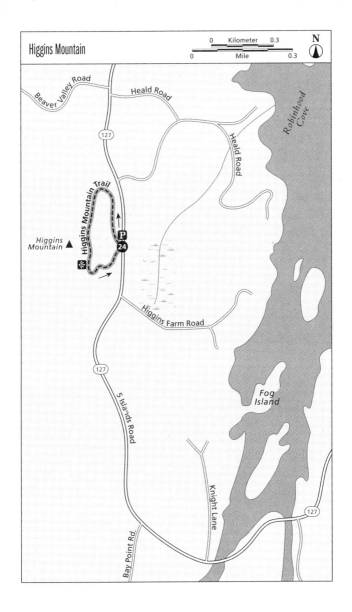

Miles and Directions

0.0   Start from the trail that heads north from the trailhead.

0.2   The trail climbs gently at first then steeply up bare rock to the long, semi-open top of Higgins Mountain.

0.3   As you hike across the mountaintop, views of the coast and surrounding islands open up.

0.4   Begin to descend.

0.6   Arrive back at the trailhead.

25 Josephine Newman Sanctuary

The Josephine Newman Sanctuary is on a finger of land that bisects the southern reaches of Robinhood Cove. The sanctuary's trails loop through the woods past a waterfall, old stone walls, piney woods, low boggy ground, rocky ridges, and a mile of shoreline that includes a reversing falls in the narrowest section of Robinhood Cove.

Start: Trailhead at south end of parking area
Distance: 2.4-mile loop
Approximate hiking time: 2 hours
Difficulty: Easy
Best season: May–Oct
Trail surface: Woodland path
Land status: Josephine Newman Audubon Sanctuary
Nearest town: Georgetown
Other users: None

Water availability: None
Canine compatibility: No dogs allowed
Fees and permits: None
Maps: *DeLorme: Maine Atlas & Gazetteer* maps 6 and 7; USGS Phippsburg and Boothbay Harbor
Trail contact: Maine Audubon, (207) 781-2330, http://maine audubon.org/find-us/josephine -newman-audubon-sanctuary

Finding the trailhead: From exit 31A on I-295, take ME 196 through Topsham 3.2 miles. Merge onto US 1 north and drive 8.1 miles to Woolwich. Exit onto ME 127 south and drive 8.7 miles to Georgetown village. ME 127 turns left and drops down to a bridge over Robinhood Cove. Across the bridge, drive 0.1 mile and turn right onto the Josephine Newman Sanctuary driveway at the small—and hard to see—sign. If you come to a second bridge, you've gone too far. Drive 0.1 mile to the parking area at the end of the driveway. The trailhead is at the south end of the parking area. GPS: N43 48.037' / W69 45.049'

The Hike

This hike follows several of the sanctuary's trails, the first being the Horseshoe Trail across a meadow and into the woods. The trail parallels Robinhood Cove, visible through the trees. Beyond the southern end of the cove, the trail follows a stream to a waterfall, then crosses to the east past several stone walls.

You then follow the Rocky End Trail toward Robinhood Cove. Be sure not to take the blue-blazed trail that leads south into Berry Woods Preserve. The Rocky End Trail drops down a rocky hill beside a stone wall to the shore of Robinhood Cove. The trail turns north, following the shore. There is a short side trail that leads out onto a rocky spit of land with fine views of the cove.

The trail climbs away from the cove. Turn right onto the Geology Trail, which drops back down to Robinhood Cove. The trail passes a rock face of dark and white rock. As Robinhood Cove narrows, the bluff the trail follows rises. The forest is dominated by mature pines. Far below, at the narrowest point of the cove, is a small reversing falls.

The trail climbs back up toward the trailhead, passing a marshy area. Throughout the sanctuary are benches to sit on and contemplate the view or soak in the sounds and scents of the woods and shore. After enjoying the contemplative quiet of this hike, you may want to continue south on ME 127 to the nearby beaches at Reid State Park.

Miles and Directions

0.0 Start from the trailhead at the south end of the parking area. In 400 feet you come to a large sign with a map and other information. Bear left onto the Horseshoe Trail.

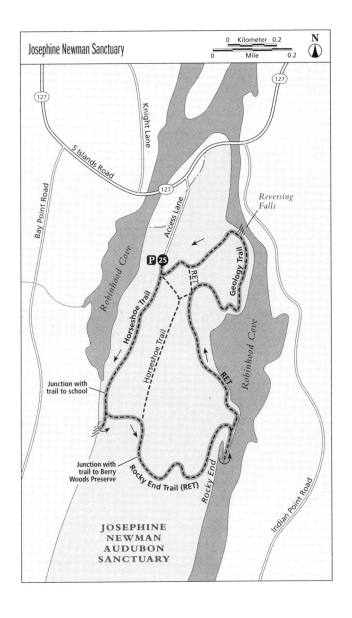

Josephine Newman Sanctuary

0 Kilometer 0.2

0 Mile 0.2

N

127

127

Knight Lane

5 Islands Road

127

Access Lane

Reversing Falls

Bay Point Road

Robinhood Cove

P 25

RET

Geology Trail

Horseshoe Trail

Horseshoe Trail

Robinhood Cove

RET

Junction with trail to school

Junction with trail to Berry Woods Preserve

Rocky End Trail (RET)

Rocky End

Indian Point Road

JOSEPHINE NEWMAN AUDUBON SANCTUARY

0.4 The Horseshoe Trail crosses a meadow and enters the woods along Robinhood Cove. Pass a side trail that leads west to Georgetown Elementary School.

0.5 A short side trail leads to a waterfall at the head of a narrow valley. The Horseshoe Trail turns east and follows an old stone wall.

0.6 Turn right onto the Rocky End Trail.

0.7 Turn left at the intersection. The trail that continues south connects with Berry Woods Preserve. This junction is unmarked and both trails are blazed blue.

0.9 The trail crosses over a hill, following a stone wall to Robinhood Cove, then turns north along the cove.

1.1 A side trail leads 400 feet out a rocky point.

1.7 Turn right onto the Geology Trail.

2.1 A rough side trail leads down to a reversing falls on Robinhood Cove.

2.3 Turn right on the Horseshoe Trail to return to the trailhead.

2.4 Arrive back at the trailhead.

26 Berry Woods

The Gamble Trail leads west over a low, wooded ridge to the Kennebec River. The channel of the Kennebec is broken by Marr and Lamb Islands—the main flow of the river is west of Marr Island. In the quiet shallows on the east side of the river, ducks and waterbirds are common. Few buildings break up the view.

Start: Trailhead at east end of parking area

Distance: 2.7 miles out and back

Approximate hiking time: 2 hours

Difficulty: Easy

Best season: May–Oct

Trail surface: Woodland path

Land status: Berry Woods Preserve

Nearest town: Georgetown

Other users: None

Water availability: None

Canine compatibility: No dogs allowed

Fees and permits: None

Maps: *DeLorme: Maine Atlas & Gazetteer* map 6; USGS Phippsburg

Trail contact: The Nature Conservancy, www.nature.org/our initiatives/regions/northamerica/unitedstates/maine

Finding the trailhead: From exit 31A on I-295, take ME 196 through Topsham 3.2 miles. Merge onto US 1 north and drive 8.1 miles to Woolwich. Exit onto ME 127 south and drive 8.7 miles to Georgetown village. Where ME 127 turns left, go straight onto Bay Point Road and drive 0.9 mile. The trailhead parking is on the right. The trailhead is at the east end of the parking area. GPS: N43 47.516' / W69 45.478'

The Hike

The Gamble Trail leads toward the Kennebec River across low, rocky ridges. In several places storm-damaged trees lie strewn about. In the sunlight new growth, including blueberries, abound. After dropping down off a low hill, the trail follows an abandoned road south through mossy lowlands.

Watch for the Kennebec River Lookout Trail on the right. It can be easy to miss. This trail down to the shore of the Kennebec River is wide, descending steadily through a mixed forest. On the shore of the river, there is a lookout with fine views up and down the Kennebec. This is not the main channel of the river, but a shallow side channel. The main channel is on the west side of Marr Island. Looking upstream, you can see the wider main channel and Phippsburg on the far side.

There are few buildings in sight to break up the scene: rocky islands covered with thick evergreens, the shoreline overhung with oaks reaching out to the light over the water, dark river water with ducks bobbing quietly. Watch, too, for herons and ospreys.

On the return hike, follow the Gamble Loop through forest still regenerating with many small trees and old roads. You can also follow the Woodex Trail across Bay Point Road to the Wilson Trail. This trail passes the north end of Wilson Pond and loops around near Robinhood Cove. A blue-blazed trail connects the Wilson Trail to the trails in the Josephine Newman Sanctuary.

Miles and Directions

0.0 Start from the trailhead at the east end of the parking area. In 200 feet, pass on the left the Woodex Right-of-Way Trail

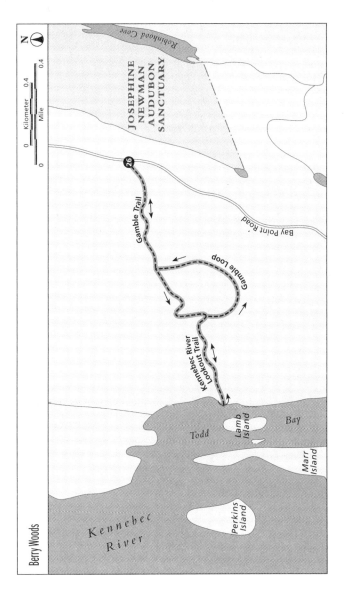

Berry Woods

JOSEPHINE
NEWMAN
AUDUBON
SANCTUARY

Robinhood Cove

Gamble Trail

Gamble Loop

Bay Point Road

Kennebec River
Lookout Trail

Todd

Bay

Lamb
Island

Marr
Island

Kennebec
River

Perkins
Island

N

Kilometer   0   0.4

Mile   0   0.4

26

(which loops back and crosses Bay Point Road, giving access to the trails in that section of Berry Woods Preserve).

0.5   The Gamble Trail ends at the Gamble Loop Trail. Bear right.

0.8   The trail drops down to an old woods road heading south. Turn right onto the Kennebec River Lookout Trail.

1.2   Arrive at the Kennebec River. To complete the hike, return the way you came to the Gamble Loop Trail.

1.6   Turn right onto the Gamble Loop Trail.

2.2   Turn right onto the Gamble Trail to return to the trailhead.

2.7   Arrive back at the trailhead.

Hike Index

Berry Woods, 119

Bradbury Mountain, 70

Burnt Meadow Mountain, 52

Cox's Head, 99

Cutts Island, 15

Douglas Mountain, 44

Giant's Stairs, 83

Hamilton Audubon Sanctuary, 87

Harpswell Cliffs, 79

Higgins Mountain, 111

Josephine Newman Sanctuary, 115

Kennebunk Plains, 28

Long Reach Preserve, 75

Mount Agamenticus, 24

Mount Cutler, 48

Carson Trail, 32

Rattlesnake Mountain, 60

Saco Heath, 40

Seawall Beach, 107

Spirit Pond, 103

Sprague Pond Loop, 95

Thorne Head, 91

Timber Point, 36

Two Lights State Park, 56

Vaughan Woods, 19

Wolfe's Neck Woods, 64

About the Author

Greg Westrich is the author of two previous hiking guides published by Falcon, and is currently working on several others. He plans to complement *Hiking Maine* with pocket guides to each of Maine's regions. Greg has also published more than fifty articles and stories in newspapers, magazines, and anthologies. He has an MFA in Creative Writing from the University of Southern Maine's Stonecoast Program. Greg lives in Glenburn with his wife, Ann, and their two children.

What's So Special about Unspoiled, Natural Places?

Beauty   Solitude   Wildness   Freedom   Quiet   Adventure
Serenity   Inspiration   Wonder   Excitement
Relaxation   Challenge

There's a lot to love about our treasured public lands, and the reasons are different for each of us. Whatever your reasons are, the national **Leave No Trace** education program will help you discover special outdoor places, enjoy them, and preserve them—today and for those who follow. By practicing and passing along these simple principles, you can help protect the special places you love from being loved to death.

The Principles of **Leave No Trace**

- Plan ahead and prepare
- Travel and camp on durable surfaces
- Dispose of waste properly
- Leave what you find
- Minimize campfire impacts
- Respect wildlife
- Be considerate of other visitors

Leave No Trace is a national nonprofit organization dedicated to teaching responsible outdoor recreation skills and ethics to everyone who enjoys spending time outdoors.

To learn more or to become a member, please visit us at www.LNT.org or call (800) 332-4100.

Leave No Trace, P.O. Box 997, Boulder, CO 80306

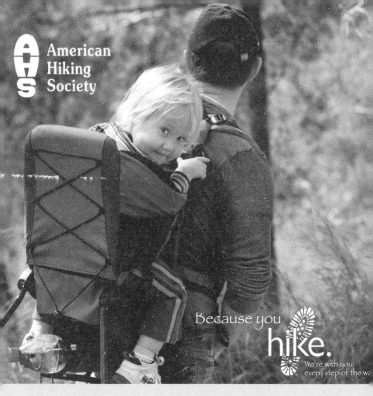

American Hiking Society

Because you
hike.
We're with you
every step of the way

American Hiking Society is the only national voice for hikers—dedicated to promoting and protecting America's hiking trails, their surrounding natural areas, and the hiking experience.

At American Hiking Society, we work hard so you can play! We advocate for families who love to hike, and we support communities who are creating new opportunities for your trail family to get outside. Hiking is a great way to bond with your kids, parents, grandparents, neighbors, or even furry friends.

Come with us on the trail and listen to the sweet sound of bird songs and look high into the boughs of old oak trees. We'll help you develop an active lifestyle, learn about the wonders of nature, and become a steward of your favorite trails. So grab your hiking shoes, a well-stocked daypack, partner, kids, friends, parents, and dogs— and get outdoors!

AMERICAN HIKING SOCIETY'S
FAMILIES on FOOT

Become a member of the national hiking community
at www.americanhiking.org. Join today!